# The Art of English

# Grammar

## Practice Workbook

## Jenny Pearson

The Art of English Grammar Practice Workbook

Jenny Pearson

Kivett Publishing

ISBN: 978-1-941691-36-6

Nonfiction > Language Arts > Grammar

Juvenile > Language Arts > Grammar

# TABLE OF CONTENTS

# INTRODUCTION

This book provides more than 50 grammar lessons. Each lesson includes a concise explanation, examples, and practice exercises. The answer to every exercise is available at the back of the book. The grammar rules in this book follow the conventions of American English. Topics include:

- parts of speech
- sentence structure
- commonly confused words
- subject-verb agreement
- dangling modifiers
- pronoun problems
- tense and mood
- active vs. passive voice
- colons and semicolons
- quotation marks and apostrophes
- action and linking verbs
- adverbs and adjectives
- comparative and superlative
- concrete vs. abstract
- possessive vs. singular
- capitalization and punctuation
- types of sentences
- run-ons and fragments
- complements
- prepositions
- conjunctions and interjections

# COMMON NOUNS (easy)

A **common noun** is a generic word that refers to a person, place, or thing. Note that an idea is a common noun because an idea is a type of thing. A common noun is not capitalized unless it begins a sentence.

- Common person examples: mother, judge, pal, athlete.
- Common place examples: bank, forest, station, aisle.
- Common thing examples: phone, diamond, course, grammar.
- Common idea examples: concept, principle, law, guess.

**Directions**: Circle the common nouns.

1) The children had fun flying a kite at the beach on a windy day.

2) Shiny earrings will look great with the dark blue blouse.

3) One rule at the park is for every dog to be on a leash.

4) Students looking for a quiet place to work often visit the library.

5) The doctor said, "Drink one cup every morning for three weeks."

6) Out of curiosity, exactly how did the cows escape from the corral?

7) Please bring the following items to the game: glove, shoes, and hat.

8) The invitation included the date and time, but not the location.

9) Yesterday, the food in the cafeteria was much tastier than usual.

10) The hiker followed the path through the woods and under a bridge.

11) "Good evening," said the girl. "At what time does the show start?"

12) A few hours after the rain stopped, the sun was beginning its ascent.

13) In the beginning, the movie was boring; the action came later.

14) After some thought, the sailor realized there was just one option.

# PROPER NOUNS (easy)

A **proper noun** is a word that refers to a specific person, place, or thing. A proper noun is always capitalized.

- Proper person examples: Kate (a girl's first name), William Shakespeare (an author), Spongebob (a cartoon character).
- Proper place examples: Paris (a city), Mount Everest (a mountain), Jupiter (a planet), Disneyland (a theme park).
- Proper thing examples: Apple (a cell phone brand), Saturday (a day of the week), Civil War (a war), *The Hobbit* (a book title).

**Directions:** Identify and correct the mistakes with proper nouns.

1) Our teacher, ms. jimenez, taught us about the revolutionary war.

2) Last summer we visited austin, which is the capital of texas.

3) Next year i will attend harbor middle school.

4) Her physician referred her to dr. williams, who is a specialist.

5) Our favorite place to buy fresh eggs is blueridge farms.

6) His sister was born on november 18 at st. francis hospital.

7) My grandmother lives on second avenue in phoenix, arizona.

8) I bought crest toothpaste on amazon sunday and it arrived monday.

9) Sara, lisa, and anna hope to visit the grand canyon someday.

10) In the summer, we drove to the top of pike's peak in colorado.

11) We dressed up like characters from *snow white* last halloween.

12) On thursday, dad bought me nike shoes at the mall of america.

13) Yesterday, i told mom that my brother, keith, was rude to your dad.

# PLURALS (medium)

The **plural** form of a noun refers to more than one person, place, or thing. Plurals are also used for zero (as in "no pets"). Recall that an idea is a kind of thing. Most plural nouns follow one of the following rules:

- Most plurals add <u>s</u> to the end: buildings, weeks, arrays, clues.

- If a noun ends with <u>ch</u>, <u>s</u>, <u>sh</u>, <u>ss</u>, <u>x</u>, or <u>z</u>, add <u>es</u> to the end: pouches, buses, radishes, guesses, boxes, waltzes. Beware that there are a few exceptions to this rule, like quizzes (where the <u>z</u> gets doubled) and stomachs (where the <u>ch</u> makes the <u>k</u> sound).

- If a noun ends with <u>y</u> and a consonant comes before the <u>y</u>, replace <u>y</u> with <u>ies</u>: cities, batteries, pennies. However, if a noun ends with <u>y</u> and a vowel comes before the <u>y</u>, keep the <u>y</u> and add <u>s</u>: days, monkeys, toys.

- If a noun ends with <u>o</u> and a vowel comes before the <u>o</u>, add <u>s</u>: radios, videos, igloos. However, if a noun ends with <u>o</u> and a consonant comes before the <u>o</u>, add <u>es</u>: heroes, potatoes, echoes. There are exceptions to this rule, especially with musical terms: pianos, banjos, solos. A few words have two acceptable plural spellings, such as zeros and zeroes.

- If a noun ends with <u>f</u>, change the <u>f</u> to a <u>v</u> and add <u>es</u> to the end: loaves, wolves, scarves. If a noun ends with <u>fe</u>, change the <u>f</u> to a <u>v</u> and add <u>s</u> to the end: knives, wives. Beware that there are a few exceptions to these rules: safes, roofs, proofs.

- Some nouns are the same whether they are singular or plural: fish, sheep, aircraft, moose, trout, buffalo. (Although this is common with animals, not all animals follow this rule: lions, monkeys, horses.)

- For nouns with Latin roots ending with <u>us</u>, change <u>us</u> to <u>i</u>: cacti, nuclei. For nouns with Latin roots ending with <u>um</u>, change <u>um</u> to <u>a</u>: data, curricula. For nouns with Latin roots ending with <u>a</u>, change <u>a</u> to <u>ae</u>: larvae, antennae. For nouns with Latin roots ending with <u>is</u>, change <u>is</u> to <u>es</u>: axes, analyses. For nouns with Latin roots ending with <u>on</u>, change <u>on</u> to <u>a</u>: phenomena, criteria.
- For some irregular nouns, vowels change to <u>e</u>'s: men, feet, teeth.
- A few irregular plurals do not follow any of the rules listed above: children, dice, people.

**Directions**: Write the plural form of each noun.

| | | |
|---|---|---|
| 1) television | 2) valley | 3) deer |
| 4) branch | 5) tomato | 6) leaf |
| 7) ratio | 8) baby | 9) sprinkler |
| 10) woman | 11) life | 12) trio |
| 13) salmon | 14) address | 15) pony |
| 16) hoof | 17) goose | 18) radius |
| 19) essay | 20) tax | 21) mouse |
| 22) bonus | 23) avocado | 24) half |
| 25) chapter | 26) medium | 27) leash |
| 28) alumnus | 29) belief | 30) vertebra |
| 31) ox | 32) virus | 33) index |

# COLLECTIVE NOUNS (medium)

A **collective noun** is a word that refers to a group of people, animals, places, or things. Examples of collective nouns include crowd (which consists of spectators), herd (a group of cows), range (a series of mountains), and bouquet (an arrangement of flowers). Note that a collective noun is singular. For example, in the phrase "pack of wolves," the collective noun is pack. Although there are multiple wolves in a pack, the term **pack** is singular because it refers to a single group.

**Directions:** Circle the collective nouns.

1) The basketball team has a specific set of drills to practice.

2) A litter of puppies enjoyed playing in a pile of leaves.

3) The battleship's crew is the most experienced in the entire fleet.

4) After a loud noise, a flock of birds flew out of the forest.

5) She chose to walk up a flight of stairs instead of riding the elevator.

6) The family went inside when a swarm of bees approached the house.

7) Management was concerned that the workers would form a union.

8) A chain of many islands is called an archipelago.

9) The students in the music class were divided into duets and quartets.

10) He has a stamp collection and a personal library of vintage books.

11) Only a single bale of hay remained to feed the livestock.

12) Profits increased when the two companies formed an alliance.

13) The observatory directed its array of telescopes at a distant galaxy.

14) A panel of experts will report to the local government on Monday.

# PRONOUNS (challenge)

A **pronoun** is a word that refers to a noun that was already used in the same sentence or a previous sentence. A common use of a pronoun is to help avoid repeating a person's name. For example, consider the sentence, "When Mrs. Smith saw the dress, she wondered how it would fit on her." The pronouns in this sentence are **she**, **it**, and **her**. If not for these pronouns, the sentence would repeat the woman's name multiple times: "When Mrs. Smith saw the dress, Mrs. Smith wondered how the dress would fit on Mrs. Smith." Using pronouns helps to avoid repeating the woman's name.

There are many different kinds of pronouns:

- A **personal pronoun** refers to a person, animal, or thing: I, me, we, us, you, he, him, she, her, it, they, them. Example: **I** gave the purse to **her**." **I** and **her** are pronouns because each could be replaced with a noun (as in "**Kelly** gave the purse to **Rachel**"). As a counterexample, in the sentence, "**I** brought **her** purse," **her** functions as an adjective (not a pronoun) because it modifies the purse.

- A **possessive pronoun** indicates a sense of belonging: mine, ours, yours, his, hers, its, theirs. (It is considered incorrect to use apostrophes with these pronouns.) Example: This soup is **his**. **His** is a pronoun because it serves the function of a noun. As a counterexample, in the sentence, "This is **his** soup," **his** functions as an adjective (not a pronoun) because it modifies the soup.

- An **interrogative pronoun** is used to ask a question: what, which, who, whom, whose. Example: **Who** forgot to put the milk in the refrigerator? (**Who** asks a question and refers to a person.)

- A **demonstrative pronoun** points out a particular noun: this, that, these, those. Example: **These** are juicy apples. (**These** refers to particular apples.) As a counterexample, in the sentence, "**These** apples are juicy," **these** functions as an adjective (not a pronoun) because it modifies the apples.

- A **relative pronoun** relates one part of a sentence to another: which, who, whom, whose, that. Example: The representative with **whom** I spoke yesterday assured me that there was a money-back guarantee. (**Whom** refers to the representative.)

- A **reflexive pronoun** reflects back to a person, animal, or thing: myself, ourselves, yourself, yourselves, himself, herself, itself, themselves. Example: We owe it to **ourselves** to try our best. (**Ourselves** reflects back to **we**.)

- An **indefinite pronoun** is a pronoun that does not necessarily refer to a specific person, animal, or thing: any, none, few, one, each, some, all, both, either, neither, several, many, most, less, little, everyone, everything, someone, something, anyone, anything, nobody, nothing, other, others, another, such, much, plenty, enough. Example: I have **something** for you in the trunk of my car. (**Something** refers to an unspecified item in the trunk.) Beware that some pronouns can be used as an adjective or as a pronoun. It is a pronoun if it could be replaced by a noun, and it is an adjective if it modifies a noun. For example, in the expression, "**Many** are pleased with the outcome," **many** is a pronoun because it could be replaced with a noun (as in "**Teachers** are pleased with the outcome"). As a counterexample, in the expression, "**Many** people are pleased with the outcome," **many** is an adjective because it modifies the noun **people** (in this case, it would not make sense to replace **many** with a noun like **teachers**).

**Directions:** Circle each pronoun and indicate which kind it is.

1) The jacket that I had found on the floor last week was definitely his.

2) Those were the most colorful patterns that anyone could find.

3) She said, "The blue bicycle is mine and the red bicycle is yours."

4) What is the matter with me? Nothing is the matter.

5) Can you believe it? We made this from scratch by ourselves today.

6) They ate dinner at the restaurant on the hill. Theirs is the best soup.

7) That is ridiculous. I doubt there is anyone who would believe it.

8) Please tell us if there is anything we can do to help you.

9) Those were the sweetest yams that I had ever tasted.

10) You should feel good about yourselves. Few could have done better.

11) The dog running around without a leash is not ours. Whose is it?

12) Only a few solutions have mistakes in them. The others are perfect.

13) The customer for whom she baked this cake is waiting outside now.

14) Which orange is the juiciest? That is the one I want to eat.

# POSSESSIVE (medium)

A **<u>possessive noun</u>** includes an apostrophe (') and indicates a sense of belonging. A **<u>singular</u>** noun refers to a single person, animal, place, or thing, whereas a **<u>plural</u>** noun refers to multiple people, animals, places, or things (or zero, as in "no students were in attendance").

- If a singular noun does not end with <u>s</u>, add <u>'s</u>: the restaurant's parking lot, Dan's bicycle, a book's cover, the caterpillar's thorax.

- If a plural noun does not end with <u>s</u>, add <u>'s</u>: the children's books. (Since most plurals end with <u>s</u>, this rule is for irregular plurals.)

- If a singular noun ends with <u>s</u>, a common rule is to add <u>'s</u> unless the <u>'s</u> would make pronunciation troublesome (in which case, just add <u>'</u> without the extra <u>s</u>): the bus's horn, Chris's grade, Venus's atmosphere, Moses' father (since Moses's is harder to pronounce), Archimedes' principle (instead of Archimedes's principle). Beware that some people follow a different convention, which is to add <u>'</u> without the extra <u>s</u> for all singular nouns that end in <u>s</u>. Technically, it is not incorrect to write Chris' grade or Venus' atmosphere (instead of Chris's grade or Venus's atmosphere).

- If a plural noun ends with <u>s</u>, add <u>'</u> without an additional <u>s</u>: the twin girls' bracelets, five elephants' trunks, the Jones' home (which is owned by Mr. and Mrs. Jones).

- Treat a collective noun as singular: the band's singer, the class's chalkboard. (An exception is made when there are multiple units. For example, if there are three different bands, the bands' singers would refer to the singers of all three bands.)

- When two nouns possess a single object, only use an apostrophe for the second noun: Mark and Rita's dog. When two nouns each possess objects, use an apostrophe for both nouns: Mark's and Rita's fathers (which collectively refers to Mark's father and Rita's father, whereas Mark and Rita's father would mean that Mark and Rita have the same father).

- Recall that possessive pronouns do not use an apostrophe: ours, yours, his, hers, its, theirs. (Note: **it's** is a contraction for **it is**, while **its** is a possessive pronoun, as in "The dog wagged **its** tail.")
- Beware that some common objects do not use an apostrophe: door knob (instead of door's knob), windshield wipers (instead of windshield's wipers), house key (instead of house's key).

**Directions:** Identify and correct the mistakes with possessive nouns.

1) Paul had left the dogs leash in the back of his dads truck.

2) All of the boys moms waved goodbye as the school bus drove away.

3) The girls changed their clothes in the womens locker room.

4) Alexis asked, "Did anyone find the boss wifes purse last night?"

5) She could hardly believe that her older brothers room was now hers.

6) Many of the forests trees were over one hundred feet tall.

7) The students golf bags have the schools name printed on their sides.

8) My aunt and uncle only car is in the shop having its radiator fixed.

9) Yesterday, I got both the pitcher and shortstop autographs.

10) The boys and girls first floor bathrooms are both out of order.

11) One of the Jeffersons cats slept in Mr. Kings desk drawer.

12) Zach and Kayla twin daughters graduated from college in May.

13) Ms. Bailey and Ms. Hopes pools both have diving boards.

14) Her cousins will be defendants at the peoples court tomorrow.

# ABSTRACT NOUNS (medium)

A **concrete noun** can be seen, heard, smelled, touched, or tasted. An **abstract noun** is an idea (or concept), belief, or quality that can not be detected through the five senses.

- Concrete noun examples: moon, bell, perfume, velvet, chocolate.
- Abstract noun examples: independence, religion, honesty.

**Directions:** Indicate whether each boxed noun is concrete or abstract.

1) Vibrant colors in the painting brought joy to those who viewed it.

2) He received his first penalty when the referee blew his whistle.

3) What was that fragrance? It brought much delight to her nose.

4) A cool breeze made the evenings seem bearable in the summer.

5) He felt so much disgust at the sour taste that he spit the fruit out.

6) The woman finally mustered enough courage to stand up for herself.

7) Looking through a telescope, he saw a nebula that looked like a crab.

8) This new style of the fashion industry involves much creativity.

9) We learned about government and religion in history today.

10) She said, "I am in love with the design on the back of your jacket."

11) Where will we go on our vacation? Is it a surprise?

12) With enough wisdom, they would end the war and make peace.

13) The jury decided that the defendant had, in fact, broken the law.

# ACTION VERBS (easy)

A **verb** is a word that expresses an action, an event, or a state. An **action verb** expresses an action. Physical actions involve a person, animal, or object doing something physical, whereas mental actions do not.

- Physical action examples: climb, accelerate, bark, put, call, talk.
- Mental action examples: imagine, care, analyze, like, dream.

**Directions:** Circle each verb and indicate if it is physical or mental.

1) Believe it or not, Carlos swims very fast. He won a race last week.

2) Please paint your room tomorrow. Choose the colors today.

3) Sheila wished for more time to play games with her friends.

4) My father told me not to worry about my dentist appointment.

5) Claire hopes that she dances well in next month's competition.

6) I memorized the definitions yesterday. I already forgot half of them.

7) We stared at each other for several moments without blinking.

8) They planned to meet in the clubhouse soon after the bell rang.

9) Gabe's mother said, "Please remember to set the table before dinner."

10) After escaping from the danger, he needed a good place to hide.

11) They decided to enjoy the last day of their vacation together.

12) Stop weeping. Breathe deeply. Think about a happy memory.

13) Surprised? No. I expected to confuse their names at some point.

14) We sympathized with the girl who yelled, "Stop judging me."

15) The customer wants to speak with a manager regarding a refund.

# TRANSITIVE VERBS (medium)

A **transitive verb** is an action verb that takes a direct object, which means that it has an effect on a person or thing. A transitive verb gets its name because it transfers its action to a person or thing. An **intransitive verb** is an action verb that does not take a direct object. Some action verbs are transitive, while others are intransitive.

In the examples below, the boxed word is a **transitive verb** because it takes a direct object.

- The ice skater │lifted│ his partner over his head. (Who was lifted? His partner. The object of the verb **lifted** is his **partner**.)
- The chef │sliced│ onions on the cutting board. (What was sliced? The onions. The object of the verb **sliced** is the noun **onions**.)

In the examples below, the boxed word is an **intransitive verb** because it does not take a direct object.

- The acrobat │fell│ onto the netting below. (Who fell? The acrobat fell; however, acrobat is the subject of the sentence, not a direct object of the verb **fell**.)
- The egg │broke│ when it fell on the counter. (What broke? The egg broke; however, egg is the subject of the sentence, not a direct object of the verb **broke**.)

Beware that some verbs can be used either in a transitive sense or in an intransitive sense, like the example below.

- He │opened│ the door. (Here, **door** is the object of the verb **opened**.)
- The door suddenly │opened│. (Here, **door** is the subject of the sentence, not a direct object of the verb **opened**.)

18

**Directions:** Circle each verb and indicate whether or not it is transitive. If the verb is transitive, identify the direct object of the verb.

1) This morning, my nephew accidentally spilled milk on my toast.

2) Heather received her driver's license. Now she drives to school.

3) Please sit down and read the next two chapters of your textbook.

4) Nick called Mr. Gomez last night. They spoke for half an hour.

5) He set the map on the table carefully before pacing back and forth.

6) Don't walk! Run! The movie begins two minutes from now.

7) The coach chose Pria for team captain. She agreed with the decision.

8) William taught the secret handshake to Luke before the meeting.

9) Don't give up yet. The other team's best player injured her foot.

10) Peter threw my grandfather's magazines in the garbage can.

11) Elizabeth sent Stephen his mother's favorite recipe book.

12) I remember a time when Caleb and Josh caught a dozen catfish.

13) The dog that Maddie brought home ate the cat's food today.

# TO BE (easy)

Not all verbs express action. Some verbs express being. This is most obvious when the verb involves a form of **to be**:

- Single word forms of to be: am, are, is, be, being, been, was, were.
- Multiple word forms of to be: has been, have been, had been, may be, might be, will be, would be, should have been, would have been, could have been, will have been, etc.

**Directions**: Circle the forms of the verb **to be**.

1) Where were you yesterday? Your mother was worried about you.

2) It had been several years since he had eaten cereal for breakfast.

3) I am not sure about my answer. Were you able to figure it out?

4) One problem with being nice is that people tend to take advantage.

5) This could be a new record. The crowd is cheering them on.

6) Excuse me, sir. Do you have any idea where we're going?

7) I'm writing to ask if you will be joining us at the restaurant tonight.

8) Please be prepared when I pick you up for practice tomorrow.

9) Why is it so cold in this room? How are we supposed to think clearly?

10) It wouldn't be the first time that she would embarrass her uncle.

11) You're right; I've been stressing out for no reason.

12) I am not sure if this is the place where we are supposed to be.

13) It'd be great to know if they're already on their way here.

14) That must have been the hundredth time that he had been late.

# LINKING VERBS (medium)

A **linking verb** connects the subject with the rest of the sentence without showing any action.

- The different forms of **to be** are linking verbs: am, are, is, be, being, been, was, were, has been, may be, should have been, etc.
- The verbs **become** and **seem** are always linking verbs.
- Some verbs are sometimes linking verbs and sometime action verbs, depending on how they are used in the sentence. Examples include look, appear, sound, smell, feel, touch, taste, grow, remain, stay, prove, and turn.

A **linking verb** can be replaced with a form of **to be** in such a way that the new sentence makes sense. Compare these examples:

- The cabin looked small. "The cabin was small" makes sense. Here, **looked** is a linking verb; it does not show action.
- He looked to his left. "He was to his left" does not make sense. Here, **looked** is an action verb; it shows action.

**Directions:** Indicate whether the boxed word is a linking or action verb.

1) The nurse sounded sincere.

2) That movie seems scary.

3) I never tasted Meg's lasagna.

4) He felt sleepy after work.

5) They were all in a good mood.

6) We turned right at the signal.

7) Please remain calm.

8) These peaches smell fresh.

9) Mark Twain became famous.

10) Mr. Jay grew a mustache.

11) We proved him wrong.

12) Her leg looks fine now.

# HELPING VERBS (challenge)

A **helping verb** (also called an **auxiliary verb**) gives additional support to a main verb, helping to express the tense, mood, or voice of the verb.
- Primary helping verbs: to be, to do, to have.
- **Modal helping verbs** express possibility or necessity: may, might, can, could, would, should, will, shall, must.

Following are examples of how helping verbs can be used:
- Examples of helping to show tense: she **is** writing, she **was** writing, she **will be** writing, she **had been** writing.
- Examples of helping to show mood: it **has** begun (indicative; states a fact), **don't** go (imperative; gives a command), **do** you care? (interrogative; asks a question, expressing uncertainty).
- Examples of helping to show a passive voice: it **was** written by Raj Patel, it **will be** written by Raj Patel. (Compare with the active voice: Raj Patel wrote it, Raj Patel will write it.)
- Examples of helping to express possibility or necessity: **might** happen, **can** win, **must** be, **should** work.

**Directions:** Circle the helping verbs and indicate what they show.

1) Guests were waiting in the lobby.

2) We did not receive a discount.

3) It had been raining earlier.

4) She was given several chances.

5) He will be walking to school.

6) You may use the restroom.

7) This could be the missing link.

8) Everyone will be seen.

9) I have been babysitting all day.

10) You must stay in the line.

11) We will visit the museum soon.

12) Didn't you enjoy the story?

# VERBALS (challenge)

A **verbal** is a form of a verb that functions as another part of speech, such as a noun or adjective. Verbals include participles, gerunds, and infinitives. A **participle** is a present or past tense form of a verb that often functions as an **adjective** (meaning that it modifies a noun) when it is not part of a compound verb. A **present participle** ends with **ing**, whereas a **past participle** ends with **ed** (like walked), **d** (like sold), **t** (like brought), **en** (like fallen), or a variety of other irregular endings (like came or stung). A **gerund** (pronounced with a **j**) is a form of a verb that ends with **ing** and functions as a **noun**. If the gerund belongs to a noun or pronoun, use the possessive. For example, write "The baby's crying drove me crazy" (instead of "The baby crying drove me crazy").

- Present participle example: "She has a soothing voice"; **soothing** serves as an adjective to describe the noun **voice**. Second example: "She is calming the customers"; **is calming** is a compound verb. Third example: "Sweating from his workout, the man headed straight for the shower"; **sweating** serves as an adjective to describe the noun **man**.

- Past participle example: "I ate scrambled eggs"; **scrambled** serves as an adjective to describe the noun **eggs**. Second example: "She has scrambled the letters"; **has scrambled** is a compound verb.

- Gerund example: "I love reading"; **reading** serves as a noun; **reading** is the object of the verb **love**. Second example: "Dancing burns calories"; **dancing** serves as a noun; **dancing** is the subject of the verb **burns**. Third example: "His complaining got on my nerves"; **complaining** serves as a noun; **his complaining** is the subject of the verb **got**.

**Directions:** Identify the participles and gerunds. For each, indicate if it functions as an adjective, noun, or part of a compound verb.

1) Your checkered pants are soaking in the washing machine.

2) Boating turned out to be as easy as the charming man had claimed.

3) We enjoyed vacationing until coyotes stole our camping supplies.

4) The man waving his hands is the coach for our school's rowing team.

5) Screaming in delight, the kids ran to the frozen lemonade stand.

6) Your shouting woke me up from a terrifying nightmare. Thank you.

7) Surprised by the news, the man slowly sat down on the padded chair.

8) The tree leaning to the left was planted by my youngest daughter.

9) Please hand the sealed envelope to the person sitting to your right.

10) Veronica's singing was an unexpected delight at tonight's party.

11) The lady had said, "Set the frosted glasses on the dining table."

12) We like hiking, ziplining, and rafting down the roaring rapids.

13) Shouted words are rarely meant to create smiling faces.

# INFINITIVES (challenge)

An **infinitive** includes the word **to** plus a verb. An infinitive commonly functions as a noun, adjective, or adverb.

- Noun example: "I like to win"; **to win** serves as a noun (compare with "I like carrots," where the noun **carrots** is a direct object).

- Adjective example: "It is a snack to eat"; **to eat** serves as an adjective (compare with "It is a tasty snack," where the adjective **tasty** modifies the noun **snack**). An **adjective** modifies a noun to describe quality, quantity, or distinguishing features.

- Adverb example: "We exercise to stay in shape"; **to stay** serves as an adverb; **to stay** modifies the verb **exercise**, explaining why we exercise. An **adverb** modifies a verb, adjective, or other adverb to explain why, how much/often, when, where, to what degree, etc.

Beware that the word **to** is sometimes omitted, which makes identifying the infinitive trickier. This is called a **bare infinitive**.

- The word **to** is omitted after **modal helping verbs**: may, might, can, could, would, should, will, shall, must. For example, write "We should wait" instead of "We should to wait."

- The word **to** is omitted after **do**, **let**, **watch**, **see**, **hear**, **feel**, and a few other common verbs where it would sound funny to include the word **to** (except in passive form). For example, write "Let us play" instead of "Let us to play" and write "He made me work" instead of "He made me to work."

- The word **to** is optional after **help**, **dare**, and **bid** (except in passive form). For example, "I helped make the cake" is equivalent to "I helped to make the cake."

A **split infinitive** arises when another word is inserted between <u>to</u> and the verb. For example, "to quickly work" has a split infinitive, whereas "to work quickly" does not. In a few rare cases, a split infinitive sounds better. For example, "I want these pants to actually fit" sounds better than "I want these pants actually to fit" or "I want these pants to fit actually." In these rare cases, the split infinitive is preferred; in most cases, where a split infinitive does not sound better, a good rule of advice is to avoid it if the writing is formal (though split infinitives are generally considered more acceptable than they had been in the past).

**Directions:** Circle each infinitive and indicate if it functions as a noun, adjective, or adverb.

1) The children want to play.

2) We had supplies to purchase.

3) Dad knows the best places to fish.

4) To listen is considered polite.

5) Eat vegetables to remain healthy.

6) To relax, she listens to music.

7) There is still much work to do.

8) He came here to dance.

9) I went to the store to buy food.

10) My sister loves to skate.

**Directions:** In the blank before each infinitive, decide whether the word <u>to</u> is required, must be omitted, or is optional.

11) When the game was close, everyone watched the teams ___ play .

12) Samantha, please help me ___ clean the kitchen tomorrow.

13) "I can ___ fix any problem," the handyman said to the lady.

14) You must ___ wash your hands before coming to the dinner table.

15) We need ___ hear both sides of the story before we make a decision.

16) Did you hear my daughter ___ sing in the show last night?

# PRINCIPAL PARTS (medium)

A verb has four **principal parts**:

- The **present infinitive** is the form that would follow the word **to**. The present infinitive is the basis for the simple present tense and the simple future tense. Examples: he loves you, it will break.

- The **past tense** is used in the simple past tense. For regular verbs, the past tense ends with **ed** (like laughed). For irregular verbs, the past tense may end with **d** (like hid), **t** (like taught), **n** (like won), or a variety of other irregular endings (like grew or rang). Examples: he loved you, we called her, it broke, I rode in the car.

- The **past participle** is used in the perfect tense (present, past, or future) after **has**, **had**, or **have**. For regular verbs, the perfect participle ends with **ed** (like laughed) and is the same as the past tense. For irregular verbs, the past participle may end with **d** (like hid), **t** (like taught), **en** (like fallen), or a variety of other irregular endings (like grown or rung). Many irregular verbs have a past tense that is different from the past participle (like wore and worn), but some have the same form (like swept). Examples: he has loved you, we had called her, it will have broken, I have ridden in the car.

- The **present participle** is formed by adding **ing** to the infinitive. The present participle is used in the progressive tense and the perfect progressive tense. Examples: he is loving you, we had been calling her, it will be breaking, I have been riding in the car.

Dictionaries that list all four principal parts of verbs list them in the following order: present infinitive, past tense, past participle, present participle. Example: break, broke, broken, breaking.

**Directions:** Indicate which of the four principal parts each verb uses. For a **compound verb** (like **had looked** or **will be walking**), indicate which of the four principal parts the **main** verb uses.

1) My mother baked cookies to bring to the school on Monday.

2) When you swing the golf club, keep your eye on the golf ball.

3) I was looking for you to find out if you had watched the show yet.

4) The customer announced, "This jacket fits me perfectly."

5) People have been waiting for hours to buy Kenji's artwork.

6) Our friends had already left the restaurant when we arrived.

7) She remembers what happened the last time that they came here.

8) The sun will have risen by the time he returns with the supplies.

9) "I am telling you how I lost the key," I said, "but you won't listen."

10) Wake up. Guests have been arriving for the past half hour.

11) The detective has found a clue to Mrs. Chan's disappearance.

12) Any loose items will slide off the truck when it rounds the turn.

13) They will still be flying when the masterpiece will have sold.

# VERB TENSE (medium)

The **tense** of a verb indicates the time when the action (or state of being) occurs. There are three **verb tenses**: past tense, present tense, and future tense. Each tense is divided into four categories: simple, progressive, perfect, and perfect progressive. Note: Some grammar resources use the word **continuous** instead of **progressive**.

|  | simple | progressive | perfect | perfect progressive |
|---|---|---|---|---|
| present | show<br>shows | am showing<br>is showing<br>are showing | have shown<br>has shown | have been showing<br>has been showing |
| past | showed | was showing<br>were showing | had shown | had been showing |
| future | will show<br>shall show | will be showing | will have shown | will have been showing |

Use the **past tense** for an action that was completed (or a state of being that existed) or that was in progress at a former time.

- Use the **simple past tense** for an action that has already occurred. Example: Last month, she **proved** that a man was innocent.

- Use the **past progressive tense** for an action that was in progress in the past. Use **was/were** + the **ing** form. Example: Yesterday, she **was proving** a new theory.

- Use the **past perfect tense** for an action that occurred prior to another action. Use **had** + past participle. Example: She **had proven** four math theorems before she applied to graduate school.

- Use the **past perfect progressive** tense for an ongoing past action that was completed prior to another past action. Use **had been** + the **ing** form. Example: She **had been proving** theories for years before she became an experimentalist.

Use the **present tense** for an action that is occurring now (or a state of being as it exists now) or an action that is usual, habitual, or repeated.

- Use the **simple present tense** for an action that is current or that is usual, habitual, or repeated. Example: She **proves** math theorems every year.

- Use the **present progressive tense** for an action that is currently in progress. Use **am/is/are** + the **ing** form. Example: Now she **is proving** a new theory.

- Use the **present perfect tense** for an action that began in the past and is still current. Use **have/has** + past participle. Example: She **has proven** six of her eight theorems this year.

- Use the **present perfect progressive** tense for an action that began in the past, is currently in progress, and may continue in the future. Use **have/has been** + the **ing** form. Example: She **has been proving** theories for the past eight years.

Use the **future tense** for an action (or a state) that has not yet begun.

- Use the **simple future tense** for an action that will occur. Example: Next year, she **will prove** a new scientific theory.

- Use the **future progressive tense** for an action that will be in progress. Use **will be** + the **ing** form. Example: Next month, she **will be proving** a new theory.

- Use the **future perfect tense** for a future action that will occur prior to another action. Use **will have** + past participle. Example: She **will have proven** four math theorems before she graduates.

- Use the **future perfect progressive** tense for a future ongoing action that will be completed prior to another future action. Use **will have been** + the **ing** form. Example: Next March, she **will have been proving** theories for twelve years.

**Directions:** For each verb or **compound verb** (like **had grown** or **will be rising**), indicate if the tense is past, present, or future and also indicate if the tense is simple, progressive, perfect, or perfect progressive.

1) When school ends, we will meet at the park with our skateboards.

2) Jeff had thrown the cards away before he learned whose they were.

3) In May, you will have been attending school for ten years.

4) Last week, they were building a robot. Now they are testing it out.

5) My brothers have already scored 24 of the team's points tonight.

6) Believe it or not, we will be visiting the same small town in the fall.

7) We have been searching for my father's car keys since we woke up.

8) Eat a snack now. The game will have begun before the pizza arrives.

9) He had been reading novels for years before he wrote his first story.

10) I'm currently waiting in line. I will call you when I buy the tickets.

11) She had heard the news on the radio before she reached home.

12) When my dad retires, he will have been working for forty years.

13) Holly has found twelve of the Easter eggs this morning.

# IRREGULAR VERBS (medium)

For a **regular verb**, the past tense and past participle are formed by adding **ed** to the present infinitive. Most verbs are regular verbs.

| present infinitive | past tense | past participle | present participle |
|---|---|---|---|
| join | joined | joined | joining |

For an **irregular verb**, the past tense and past participle don't follow the usual rules. Following are a few examples.

| present infinitive | past tense | past participle | present participle |
|---|---|---|---|
| fall | fell | fallen | falling |
| grow | grew | grown | growing |
| swim | swam | swum | swimming |
| teach | taught | taught | teaching |

**Directions:** Write the past tense and past participle forms of each verb.

1) be                          2) begin

3) break                       4) catch

5) come                        6) do

7) draw                        8) drink

9) drive                       10) eat

11) feel                       12) find

13) fly                        14) freeze

15) get

16) give

17) go

18) hear

19) hide

20) keep

21) know

22) lay

23) leave

24) lie

25) pay

26) ride

27) ring

28) rise

29) say

30) see

31) seek

32) sell

33) shake

34) shrink

35) speak

36) stand

37) steal

38) swear

39) take

40) think

41) throw

42) wear

# ADJECTIVES (easy)

An **adjective** is a word that modifies a noun or pronoun (or a group of words that functions as a noun). An adjective can modify a noun by describing its qualities, by quantifying how much there is, or by distinguishing it from other nouns.

- A **descriptive adjective** describes a characteristic (color, shape, size, taste, intelligence, personality, speed, etc.) of a noun. Most adjectives are descriptive adjectives. Examples of descriptive adjectives: red, narrow, sour, wise, friendly, swift, thirsty.

- A **quantitative adjective** describes the quantity (how many or how much) of a noun. Examples of quantitative adjectives: **three** apples, **several** people, **some** sugar, **much** happiness.

- An **attributive adjective** comes directly before (or after) a noun or pronoun. Most adjectives are attributive adjectives (and are also descriptive adjectives). Examples of attributive adjectives: **messy** hair, **sleepy** kitten, **angry** tyrant. Usually, an adjective comes before a noun, but rarely an adjective can follow the noun. A **postpositive adjective** comes directly after the noun or pronoun. Example of a postpositive adjective: nothing **strange**.

- A **predicate adjective** follows a linking verb (forms of **to be** or verbs that can be replaced with a form of **to be**, such as seem, become, appear, etc.), appearing in the predicate of the sentence. Example of a predicate adjective: The game sounds **interesting**.

- A **comparative adjective** compares two nouns. Examples of comparative adjectives: smaller, funnier, louder. A **superlative adjective** indicates which of three or more nouns is the most extreme. Examples of superlative adjectives: smallest, funniest.

- A **distributive adjective** refers to a member of a group. Examples of distributive adjectives: each, every, any, either, neither.

- A **possessive adjective** indicates a sense of belonging. Examples of possessive adjectives: my, our, your, his, her, its, their, whose.

- A **demonstrative adjective** points out a particular noun. Examples of demonstrative adjectives: this, that, these, those. (These same words can also be used as demonstrative pronouns. Compare "This pencil is sharp," where **this** is an adjective, with "This is a sharp pencil," where **this** is a pronoun.)

- An **interrogative adjective** asks a question. Examples of interrogative adjectives: what, which, whose. (These words can also be used as interrogative pronouns. Compare "Which apple is ripe?" with "Which is a ripe apple?")

- A **limiting adjective** places a limit on a noun or pronoun. A limiting adjective may also be another kind of adjective, such as a quantitative, demonstrative, or possessive adjective. Examples of limiting adjectives: these, those, our, some, many, left, right.

- A **proper adjective** is an adjective formed from a proper noun. Examples of proper adjectives: Spanish, American, Olympic.

- A **participial adjective** is formed from a participle (present or past). Examples of participial adjectives: charming, tired, hidden.

- A **compound adjective** joins multiple words together using hyphens. Example of compound adjectives: hands-on, gluten-free.

- An **article** modifies a noun and thus also performs the basic function that an adjective performs (but some texts treat articles as a separate part of speech from adjectives). There are three articles: **a**, **an**, and **the**. The first two are called indefinite articles, while the last is a definite article.

**Directions:** Circle the adjectives, but do not circle articles.

1) Numerous pictures of colorful flowers were pinned to the cork board.

2) The girl with the long brown hair is the fastest runner in our class.

3) He wore a checkered shirt, denim shorts, and a pair of jogging shoes.

4) "These problems are hard," said the frustrated student.

5) I bought a dozen eggs, nonfat milk, and fresh oranges for ten dollars.

6) Your cat is friendlier than mine. My cat likes to show his sharp claws.

7) The beige jacket looks soft and fluffy. It is also expensive.

8) Whose crumbs are on the desk? This morning, that desk was clean.

9) I'm bored. Let's find something interesting to do. What sounds fun?

10) Every student in his class had messy handwriting last year.

11) One time, I drew a spiral graph. Another time, I made glass prisms.

12) Our German shepherd won first place for her good behavior.

13) He took many trips to the southern states during those years.

14) Stay calm. Be quiet. Don't make any sudden movements.

15) Your high-pitched scream woke me up from a pleasant dream.

16) He was excited. It was the most original idea he'd heard all week.

17) That shiny earring has a broken clasp, but these are fine.

18) We rode our bicycles along a winding road for several minutes.

19) My hair is messy, my clothes are wrinkled, and we will be tardy.

20) Few gamers have scored a million points in this new game.

21) Natalie will be the next French girl to receive a gold medal.

22) His coach put him on a high-calorie diet with a secret ingredient.

# ORDER OF ADJECTIVES (easy)

When multiple adjectives modify the same noun, they usually come in the following order. (Otherwise, the sentence may sound funny.)

- **Determiners** go first. These include **articles** (a, an, the), **possessive adjectives** (my, your, etc.), and **demonstrative adjectives** (this, those, etc.). Although determiners also include quantifiers, quantitative adjectives come next on the list.

- **Quantitative adjectives** (one, four, some, many, etc.) are next.

- **Opinions, qualities, and values** (beautiful, wise, cheap, polite, rough, etc.) are next.

- **Size** (small, medium, enormous, etc.) is next. Some references also include **temperature** (cold, hot, etc.) with or after size.

- **Age** (young, old, etc.) comes next.

- **Shape** (round, square, etc.) is considered next according to some references, while other references list shape with or after size (but it is a rare occasion when this makes a difference).

- **Color** (yellow, gray, etc.) is next.

- **Origin** (Spanish, etc.) and **material** (metal, glass, etc.) go next.

- **Purpose** (frying, writing, etc.) comes last.

If multiple adjectives come immediately before the noun they describe (unlike predicate adjectives), the adjectives are ordered according to the above list without using the word "and." In this case, a comma is only used if two adjectives belong to the same category. For example, "three wise men" has **three** (quantitative) come before **wise** (an opinion) with no comma, whereas "foolish, romantic man" has a comma because **foolish** and **romantic** belong to the same category (both are opinions).

**Directions:** Rewrite each sentence, putting the boxed words in the correct order.

1) He bought a green large truck.

2) antique few wooden stools are as nice as this one.

3) I love plaid soft your blanket.

4) Have you seen any purple narrow balloons?

5) cute elderly the couple made a donation to our school.

6) Please hand me paper those white towels.

7) I ate delicious English two muffins.

8) Careful. These instruments have cutting jagged metal blades.

9) Would you like red some spicy peppers?

10) My sister plays with building colorful foam blocks.

11) friendly our thoughtful neighbors baked cookies for us.

12) Celia has Christmas three ugly sweaters.

# ARTICLES (easy)

In English grammar, an **article** refers to the word **a**, **an**, or **the**.

- The **indefinite articles** (**a** and **an**) do **not** refer to a specific person, place, or thing. Use **a** before a consonant sound and use **an** before a vowel sound (regardless of how the word is spelled). Examples: a coin, an idea. Note that the letter "h" is sometimes pronounced as a consonant and is sometimes silent. Examples: a hug, a house, an hour, an heir. Use **a** before the letters "y" and "w" when they make consonant sounds. Examples: a yo-yo, a year, a walnut, a white hat. Note that the letter "u" is sometimes pronounced as a consonant (with "y") and is sometimes pronounced as a vowel. Examples: a union, a eucalyptus tree, an umpire, an umbrella. When an indefinite article is used before a letter, number, or symbol, choose the article based on how it is pronounced. Examples: a DVD, an MRI, an 8-ball, a + sign, an = sign.

- The **definite article** (**the**) refers to a specific person, place, or thing. Examples: the next game, the recreation center. Note that **the** is pronounced THUH before consonant sounds (like the dog) and is pronounced THEE before vowel sounds (like the enemy).

**Directions:** Write an **indefinite** article (either **a** or **an**) in each box.

1) ☐ onion

2) ☐ lion

3) ☐ watermelon

4) ☐ yellow hat

5) ☐ honest person

6) ☐ huge boulder

7) ☐ unlit lamp

8) ☐ unit

9) ☐ European

10) ☐ eagle

11) ☐ RF adapter

12) ☐ U-turn

# ADVERBS (medium)

An **adverb** is a word that modifies a verb or adjective. An adverb can alternatively be used to modify another adverb. An adverb can even be used to modify a phrase, clause, or an entire sentence.

- Example modifying a verb: "The boy spoke quietly"; the adverb **quietly** modifies the verb **spoke** (it describes how the boy spoke).

- Example modifying an adjective: "She is very wise"; the adverb **very** modifies the adjective **wise** (it indicates how wise she is).

- Example modifying an adverb: "They run quite fast"; the adverb **quite** modifies the adverb **fast** (the adverb **quite** indicates how fast they are, while the adverb **fast** describes how they run).

- Example modifying a sentence: "Thankfully, nobody was hurt"; the adverb **thankfully** expresses the speaker's attitude.

An adverb modifies a verb, adjective, or another adverb to explain why, how, how much, how often, when, where, to what degree, to what extent, or under which circumstances.

- An **adverb of manner** describes how the action of a verb is done. These adverbs often end with **ly**. Examples: rudely, loudly, wildly, comically, politely, ferociously, fast.

- An **adverb of degree** serves as an **intensifier**, meaning that it indicates the intensity of a verb, adjective, or another adverb. Examples: quite, very, nearly, somewhat, too, almost, so, just.

- An **adverb of place** indicates where the action of a verb occurs. Examples: inside, below, nowhere, anywhere, here, there.

- An **adverb of time** indicates when the action of a verb occurs. Examples: recently, soon, during, lately, yet, earlier, yesterday.

- An **adverb of frequency** indicates how often the action of a verb occurs. Examples: usually, seldom, never, sometimes, again.
- An **adverb of reason** explains why the action of a verb occurs. Examples: so, hence.
- An **interrogative adverb** is a word that asks a question and also functions as an adverb. Interrogative adverbs: why, where, when, how. (Other common question words do not function as adverbs.)
- A **conjunctive adverb** joins two independent clauses with closely related thoughts together. The clauses may be two separate sentences, or they can be in the same sentence using a semicolon. Example: "I needed groceries; however, I didn't have time to visit the store." Note: A multi-syllable conjunctive adverb uses a comma.

**Directions**: Circle each adverb.

1) The girl skated gracefully across.

2) We will reach my house soon. Then we can go inside.

3) Dad was too smart to make that mistake again.

4) Rick rarely visits, but he is coming tomorrow.

5) Pointing at a bee, Valerie nervously announced, "Look above."

6) Fortunately, the children were working diligently.

7) I always volunteer; hence the request seems unnecessary.

8) The car shook suddenly. We were too afraid to move.

9) Are you completely insane? He barely survived that crash.

10) Where is her phone? She typically leaves it here.

11) Why is everything broken? Even my pen doesn't work well.

12) I'm very tired; therefore, I'll just speak briefly.

# ADVERB VS. ADJECTIVE (medium)

Sometimes, it is easy to distinguish between an adjective and an adverb. For example, many adjectives have a corresponding adverb that ends with **ly**, such as the adjective **famous** and the adverb **famously**. However, it is not always so easy to distinguish between an adjective and an adverb, like the examples below. The distinction has to do with how the word is used in the sentence; an **adjective** modifies a noun, whereas an **adverb** modifies a verb, adjective, or other adverb.

- The word **slow** can function as an adjective or as an adverb. In formal writing, **slowly** is the preferred form for the adverb except in rare cases where **slow** sounds better. For example, consider "Even my watch runs slow. Why is everything so slow?" The first use of **slow** is an adverb because it modifies the verb **runs**, while the second use of **slow** is an adjective that describes **everything**.

- The word **fast** can function as an adjective or as an adverb; it is unlike the word **slow** in that "fastly" is not a real word. For example, in "Please drive fast," **fast** is an adverb because it modifies the verb **drive**, while in "The car is fast," **fast** is a predicate adjective that modifies the noun **car**.

- The word **late** can function as an adjective meaning tardy or as an adverb meaning tardily. For example, in "We are late," **late** is a predicate adjective that modifies the pronoun **we**, while in "We arrived late," **late** is an adverb that modifies the verb **arrived**.

- The word **good** is an adjective; the corresponding adverb is **well**. For example, in "This pizza is good," **good** is a predicate adjective that describes the pizza, while in "I did well," **well** is an adverb that modifies the verb **did**. An exception is made for the word **well** when it relates to a health condition or wellness; for this meaning, **well** is an adjective. For example, after surgery a person might say, "I am **well**," where in this case **well** functions as an adjective describing the health of the person talking (not as an adverb).

- Some words ending with **ly** can function as adjectives. For example, in "daily news," **daily** is an adjective, while in "It happens daily," **daily** is an adverb.

**Tip:** A **predicate adjective** follows a **linking verb** (forms of **to be** or verbs that can be replaced with a form of **to be**, such as seem, become, appear, remain, etc.), whereas an **adverb** modifies an **action verb** (or an **adjective** or other **adverb**). For example, in "We are late," **are** is a linking verb (**are** is a form of **to be**), so **late** is an adjective, while in "We arrived late," **arrived** is an action verb, so **late** is an adverb.

**Directions:** Determine if each boxed word is an adjective or an adverb.

1) Choose wisely.

2) The war was costly.

3) Will you stay late?

4) We started the quiz late.

5) She worked hard today.

6) The homework looked hard.

7) Your grandmother seems friendly.

8) Guests are here already.

9) Make a right turn at the signal.

10) Turn right at the stop sign.

11) Sit close.

12) The score is close.

13) I know this looks bad.

14) Our team played poorly.

15) This could go badly.

16) We feel bad?

17) They are good people.

18) Do well on your exam.

19) I have a good feeling about this.

20) I feel well today.

43

# DEGREES (medium)

Adjectives and adverbs can be used in three **degrees** (which refer to three forms of the word), like soft, softer, and softest.

- The **positive degree** makes a statement. The positive degree is the most common degree.

- The **comparative degree** compares a quality that is shared by exactly two nouns. The comparative degree of an adjective or adverb usually either ends with **er** (like softer) or comes after the word **more** (like more dangerous) or **less** (like less dangerous).

- The **superlative degree** compares a quality that is shared by three or more nouns. The superlative degree of an adjective or adverb usually either ends with **est** (like softest) or comes after the word **most** (like most dangerous) or **least** (like least dangerous).

Following are some rules regarding comparative and superlative forms.

- One-syllable adjectives add **er** or **est**. Example: fuller, fullest. If the positive degree ends with one vowel plus one consonant (like b**ig**), the consonant is doubled. Example: big, bigger, biggest. If the positive degree ends with a silent **e**, just add **r** or **st**. Example: wise, wiser, wisest (the **e** does not get doubled).

- Adjectives or **ly** adverbs with three or more syllables use **more** or **most**. Example: more important, most important. An exception may be made if the first syllable is **un** (as in unhappiest).

- Participial adjectives use **more** or **most**, regardless of the number of syllables. Examples: more charming, more tired.

- Two-syllable adjectives ending with **y** change the **y** to **ier** or **iest**. Example: happier, happiest. Two-syllable adverbs ending with **y** (where the exact same word can't function as an adjective) tend to use **more** or **most** instead. Example: more loudly, most loudly.

- Two-syllable adjectives ending with **ow** add **er** or **est**. Examples: shallower, shallowest.
- Two-syllable adjectives ending with **le** change the **le** or to **ler** or **lest**. Example: littler, littlest.
- Two syllable adjectives with other endings (besides **y**, **ow**, and **le**) tend to use **more** or **most**. Most two-syllable adjectives fall in this category. Example: more thoughtful, most thoughtful.
- Two-syllable adjectives ending with **er** often get used both ways (sometimes adding **er** or **est** and sometimes using **more** or **most**). For example, sincerest and most sincere are both used. However, exceptions like eager, proper, and somber only use **more** or **most**.
- Some adjectives and adverbs are **irregular**; they do not have the expected **er**/**est** or **more**/**most** usage. See the list below.
- The **superlative** degree usually includes the word **the** before it. Examples: the wisest man, the most ridiculous situation.
- To emphasize that one quality is less (rather than more), always use **less** or **least**. Examples: less full, least full.

Some common **irregular** adjectives and adverbs are listed below.

- The comparative/superlative for **good** (or **well**) are **better**/**best**.
- The comparative/superlative for **bad** are **worse**/**worst**.
- The comparative/superlative for **old** are **elder**/**eldest** when referring to the age of people, but they are **older**/**oldest** when referring to things.
- The comparative/superlative for **many** (or **much**) are **more**/**most**.
- The comparative/superlative for **far** are **farther**/**farthest** or **further**/**furthest**. (Many people prefer **farther**/**farthest** for

physical distance and **further**/**furthest** for figurative distance, but there is not universal agreement about this.)

- The comparative/superlative for **little** are **less**/**least** when **little** means "small amount of," but they are **littler**/**littlest** when **little** means "small in size." Examples: Which route lets me reach the store in the least time? She has the littlest dog I've ever seen.

The **positive degree** is used to show equivalence with the word **as**. Example: My brother is about as tall as you.

Not all adjectives and adverbs have comparative or superlative degrees; some adjectives and adverbs are **incomparable**. Examples: entire, true.

**Directions:** Write the comparative and superlative forms of each word.

1) dark

2) dangerous

3) boring

4) healthy

5) dramatic

6) polite

7) pale

8) tired

9) tidy

10) thin

11) well

12) finicky

13) spunky

14) gentle

15) gently

16) unfriendly

**Directions:** Write the appropriate degree (comparative or superlative) of the boxed word in the blank to form a grammatically correct sentence. You may need to include additional words like **the** or **more**.

17) My cousin's hair is _____ than mine. | smooth |

18) He is _____ actor we know. | famous |

19) The living room is _____ than the kitchen. | dim |

20) Greg visits _____ than Derek does. | frequently |

21) That is _____ soup on the menu. | creamy |

22) He could be _____ puppy in the world. | excited |

23) The opening is _____ than I expected. | narrow |

24) Nobody comes here _____ than I do. | often |

25) Give me _____ explanation possible. | simple |

26) My tutor speaks _____ than my teacher. | simply |

27) Please wake up _____ than you did today. | early |

28) He behaves _____ than his brother. | awkwardly |

# PREPOSITIONS (easy)

A **preposition** is a word that shows how a noun or a pronoun is related to another word (such as a verb, noun, or adjective) in the sentence.

- Many prepositions show relationships involving position, location, or direction. Examples: **under** it, **on** the desk, **through** the woods, **towards** me, **behind** us, **down** the river, **along** a path.

- Some prepositions show relationships involving time. Examples: **at** midnight, **in** the winter, **on** Saturday, **during** lunch.

- Prepositions can show possessive relationships (but beware that possessive pronouns like **my** and **his** are **not** prepositions). Examples: belongs **to** me, **with** the glasses, friend **of** ours.

- Prepositions can show how something is, was, or will be done. Examples: **with** a towel, **by** mail.

- Prepositions can show relationships involving participles. Examples: written **by** her, dying **of** thirst, filled **with** courage.

- Some prepositions show more abstract relationships. Examples: talking **about** politics, **in** a pickle, hoping **for** help, **on** my mind.

- Two prepositions can work together to show a relationship. Examples: **out of** the woods, **in for** a surprise.

- Some prepositions are compound words that combine two or more simple prepositions together into a single word. Examples: **without** gloves, **into** the lake, **throughout** the ordeal.

A preposition can relate a noun or pronoun to a verb, noun, or adjective.

- In "Stay with us," **with** links the verb **stay** to the pronoun **us**.

- In "He has a bag of chips," **of** links the nouns **bag** and **chips**.

- In "I'm good at math," **at** links the adjective **good** to the noun **math**.

A common myth is that it is grammatically incorrect to end a sentence with a preposition. There is not an actual grammar rule that prohibits this. It is more of a style choice. In general, ending a sentence with a preposition makes the writing sound less formal (which is only a problem when writing something that is expected to be formal). There are sentences that sound more natural when the preposition comes at the end. Consider the sentence, "I discovered where she came from." It may not sound as good to write, "I discovered from where she came."

**Directions:** Circle each preposition.

1) The dog chased the cat across the yard, over the fence, and up a tree.

2) Put the hammer in the toolbox and lean the shovel against the shed.

3) My mother found my jar of pennies under a blanket inside the closet.

4) The boy with the green backpack wrote a story during the holidays.

5) Lost in thought, he tripped over a can of soup and fell on the ground.

6) "I'm excited about my new job," Joann announced after dinner.

7) Birds flew through the trees, around the hill, and into the sunset.

8) For lunch, she ate a taco without cheese down by the river.

9) At the talent show, the singer before me had the voice of an angel.

10) Behind the door, I found the cat lying near a statue of a dog.

11) Please bring the medicine for my grandmother home by midnight.

12) We were cheering for you from the back of the stadium.

13) Which direction did you come from? How did you get past the dogs?

14) This award for good sportsmanship was given to me at the banquet.

15) He ran along the path that led to a lake just beyond the ridge.

# CONJUNCTIONS (easy)

A **conjunction** is a word (or a phrase) that joins words, clauses, or even sentences together. There are three main categories of conjunctions.

- **Coordinating conjunctions** are used to join words, groups of words, or sentences. Coordinating conjunctions include **and**, **or**, **but**, **nor**, **for**, **yet**, and **so**. Example: Eat fruits **or** nuts. Second example: I put money in the machine, **but** nothing came out.

- **Subordinating conjunctions** are used to join two clauses. One clause is independent and the other is dependent; the conjunction introduces the dependent clause. Examples of subordinating conjunctions include because, unless, except, while, before, after, if, whether, when, and where. Subordinating conjunctions may also be phrases like "such that" or "as soon as." Example: You may not retake an exam **unless** you have a valid excuse. Second example: He gave me a key **so that** I wouldn't have to wait outside.

- **Correlative conjunctions** are pairs of conjunctions that work together. Examples of correlative conjunctions include either/or, neither/nor, both/and, as/as, and if/then. Example: **Either** Sam will cook dinner, **or** Jim will order a pizza. Second example: **If** we work together, **then** we will have enough time to go shopping.

A common myth is that it is grammatically incorrect to begin a sentence with a coordinating conjunction like **and** or **but**. There is not an actual grammar rule that prohibits this. It is more of a style choice (though there are teachers who frown upon it). If you choose to begin a sentence with **but**, ensure that the meaning is clear. When beginning a sentence with **but**, two sentences should present contrary ideas.

**Directions:** Circle each conjunction and indicate which kind it is (coordinating, subordinating, or correlating).

1) They had chocolate and vanilla, but they were out of caramel.

2) We can either take a taxi to the zoo or ride a bus to the museum.

3) Have you been to the restaurant where the waiters wear costumes?

4) The heater was on, yet she was wearing a sweater and a jacket.

5) While you were out running errands, I received a phone call.

6) You must both complete your homework and finish your chores.

7) The bus was late this morning, so my dad drove me to school.

8) He could neither check his messages nor access the discussion forum.

9) You may play outside if you wear a jacket and rain boots.

10) He orders people around as if he were the manager.

11) After you finish studying, put your book and notes away.

12) The students quizzed each other about biology until the bell rang.

13) She not only sang for us but also showed us her guitar collection.

# INTERJECTIONS (easy)

An **interjection** is a word (or phrase) that has little or no grammatical function, but which conveys an emotion such as surprise, disgust, approval, or excitement. When it conveys strong emotion, the word often stands alone as its own sentence with an exclamation mark. When the emotion is milder, it is offset by a comma instead. An interjection does not affect the meaning of a sentence.

- Hey! You just stepped on my foot. (**Hey** is an interjection.)
- This room is bright. Oh my! (**Oh my** is an interjection.)
- Well, I'll give it a try then. (**Well** is an interjection.)

Interjections are not typically used in formal writing, but are common in dialog. For informal writing, interjections tend to be more effective when they are used in moderation.

**Directions**: Circle the interjections.

1) Aha! I caught you eating Dad's pretzels without permission.

2) He hit that ball out of the ballpark. Wow!

3) We were wondering, well, if you would like to join our club.

4) Why, that is the cutest puppy I have ever seen.

5) That was close. Whew! Remind me not to try that again.

6) Oh no! I left my homework on the table at home.

7) I would like to buy one, but, um, I don't have any money.

8) This is a library. Sh! People are trying to study.

9) "Our team won the basketball game," she said. "Yippee!"

# PARTS OF SPEECH (challenge)

There are eight main **parts of speech**: nouns, pronouns, verbs, adjectives (including articles and determiners, though some references treat these as separate parts of speech), adverbs, prepositions, conjunctions, and interjections. The characteristic feature of any part of speech is the way that it is used in a sentence.

- Example: Hey! My blue vase fell and broke. **Hey** is an interjection, **My** is a possessive adjective (or determiner), **blue** is an adjective (which modifies **vase**), **vase** is a noun, **fell** is an action verb, **and** is a coordinating conjunction, and **broke** is an action verb.
- Example: He walked slowly down the stairs. **He** is a personal pronoun, **walked** is an action verb, **slowly** is an adverb (which modifies the verb **walked**), **down** is a preposition (which relates the verb **walked** to the noun **stairs**), **the** is a definite article, and **stairs** is a plural noun (it is a person, place, or thing).

**Directions:** Indicate if each boxed word functions as a noun, pronoun, verb, adjective, adverb, preposition, conjunction, or interjection.

1) Follow the path through the forest until you reach the river.

2) Her mother became suspicious when she did her chores cheerfully.

3) Who replaced your cracked window? They did an amazing job.

4) Oh, I hadn't thought of that. Your suggestion just might work.

5) I ordered a larger size, yet the sweater is still too small.

6) He gingerly set the fragile knickknack inside the display case.

7) If someone invents a robot that does chores, I'd be happy to test it.

8) Either have these altered by noon, or buy me a new pair of pants.

9) The baby dropped her bottle on the floor again. Uh oh!

10) If you set my phone beside my wallet, you may play outside.

11) There were many bags on the floor. Why did someone take his?

12) Kimberly suddenly asked, "Where did the puppy go?"

13) Unless you learn otherwise, this is how we should do it.

14) It seems obvious, Sir, that it will not, um, fit between the posts.

15) Chicago's pizza is the best I've tasted. Boston's is almost as good.

16) He denied that the damage to the roof could be his own fault.

17) Our teacher fainted during Spanish class today.

# WORD USAGE (challenge)

A single word can sometimes function as two or more different parts of speech (like an adverb and a preposition), depending on how the word is used in a sentence, as illustrated by the following examples.

- "There is jelly **inside** the donut." Here, **inside** is a preposition that links the nouns **jelly** and **donut** (a preposition takes a noun as an object; here **donut** is the object of the preposition **inside**). "Please come **inside**." Here, **inside** is an adverb that modifies the verb **come**. (Observe that **inside** is an adverb of place.) Unlike a preposition, an adverb does not take a noun as an object.

- "Do your homework **before** your friends come over." Here, **before** primarily functions as a subordinating conjunction that joins two clauses together. "I heard that joke **before**." Here, **before** is an adverb that modifies the verb **heard**. (Observe that **before** is an adverb of time.)

**Directions:** Write two sentences for each given word, showing how the same word can function as the two indicated parts of speech.

1) Use **few** as a pronoun and also as an adjective.

2) Use **over** as a preposition and also as an adverb.

3) Use **estimate** as a noun and as a verb.

4) Use **through** as an adjective and as a preposition.

5) Use **after** as a conjunction and as a preposition.

6) Use **when** as an adverb and also as a conjunction.

7) Use **since** as a preposition and also as a conjunction.

8) Use **well** as an adverb and also as an interjection.

# CAPITALIZATION (easy)

**Capitalization** refers to writing the first letter of a word with an uppercase letter (like the Grand Canyon). Following are some rules for when to (or not to) capitalize.

- Capitalize the **first letter** of the first word of every sentence.
- Capitalize **proper nouns**. Examples: Ken Carson Jr. (a person's name), Chicago, Illinois (the name of a place), Main Street (the name of a road), Eiffel Tower (the name of a landmark), Samsung (a brand or company name), World War II (the name of a war), Christianity (a religion), Easter (a holiday). Although months (like July) and days (like Tuesday) are capitalized, seasons (like winter) are not. Capitalize a person's title only if it is used with the person's name ("Professor Epstein" vs. "my professor").
- Capitalize **proper adjectives**, which are words formed from proper nouns. Examples: British, Canadian, Olympic.
- Capitalize the pronoun **I** (but not other pronouns, like me or her) and **family names** when they are used to name people. For example, compare "Where did Mom go" (where Mom is referred to as a name) with "Where did my mom go" (where mom is a common noun). Also compare "Uncle Joe" with "my uncle."
- Capitalize the first letter of the first word of a **quotation** if the text within the quotes is a complete sentence, like "The sky is blue," but not otherwise, like "such a silly goose."
- Capitalize book or movie **titles**, like *The Cat in the Hat*. Do not capitalize articles (**a**, **an**, **the**) and certain other short words in the title, but do capitalize the first word of the title even if it is an article or a short word. Which short words should not be

capitalized? Since style guides differ on this, it depends on which style guide you use (when writing for a class where capitalization is important, the teacher may adopt a specific style guide).

- Don't capitalize the first word following a semicolon (unless it happens to be a proper noun).
- Don't capitalize the first word following a colon, except when a set of complete sentences follows the colon (or if the first word following the colon happens to be a proper noun).

**Directions:** Identify and correct the mistakes with capitalization.

1) my father's name is devon carter. he was born in wichita, kansas.

2) this homework was assigned yesterday. it is due on friday.

3) our spanish teacher visited the statue of liberty last summer.

4) on veteran's day, i met the general who lives in our neighborhood.

5) he learned about general grant in mr. dean's history class today.

6) buy these items at wal-mart: soap, shampoo, and crest toothpaste.

7) she said, "hi, dad. could you please pick us up from the library now?"

8) where did you buy your nike shoes? my dad bought them at amazon.

9) have you read *the prince and the pauper* by mark twain?

10) my aunt said, "travel west on whittier boulevard for five miles."

11) back then, uncle danny used to call you his "sweet little angel."

12) this year, easter comes in march; it usually comes in april.

13) my dad speaks the following languages: english, french, and latin.

# END PUNCTUATION (easy)

Three kinds of punctuation marks can come at the end of a sentence.

- A **period** (.) comes at the end of a **declarative sentence** (which is a statement of fact—or an opinion that is stated as if it were a fact) or at the end of an **imperative sentence** (which is a command or request that does not convey strong emotion). Most sentences end with a period; most sentences are declarative or imperative. Declarative example: Dinner will be served at seven o'clock. Imperative example: Please set the table before dinner.

- A **question mark** (?) comes at the end of a direct question, which is an **interrogative sentence**. Example: How do you feel today? (Do **not** use a question mark for an **indirect** question. Example of an indirect question: She asked if I knew how to play chess.)

- An **exclamation mark** (!), also called an exclamation point, comes at the end of an **exclamatory sentence** (which conveys strong emotion). Example: Oh no! A bug is crawling up my pant leg! Avoid using an exclamation mark if the writing is formal. For informal writing, use exclamation marks in moderation.

**Directions:** Add punctuation marks where they are needed.

1) It was foggy this morning

2) What is your favorite color

3) Are you ready for the quiz

4) "I won " he exclaimed

5) Stop   Give it back now

6) I forgot   Do you know it

7) I'm not sure about this

8) "Get out " she screamed

9) When he arrives, let me know

10) How are you   I'm fine

# ABBREVIATIONS (easy)

A period doesn't always indicate that a sentence has ended; a period is also used in many abbreviations, like a.m., Dr., or Wed. If an abbreviation ends with a period and the sentence ends with that abbreviation, don't add a second period for a declarative or imperative sentence. For a question or exclamation, however, use both punctuation marks, like "Will you be here by 6:30 p.m.?"

- Examples of abbreviations using periods: Ms., Dec., etc.
- Examples of abbreviations using multiple periods: a.m., i.e., e.g.
- Examples of abbreviations without periods: JFK, tsp, CA.

**Directions**: Rewrite each sentence, replacing each boxed word with an abbreviation. Use correct capitalization and punctuation.

1) Last spring, they went on a field trip to Houston, Texas .

2) My dental appointment is on October 24.

3) Our estimated time of arrival is 7:15 in the morning .

4) Today we will visit with Vice-President Chan.

5) We won a trip to visit Washington, District of Columbia !

6) His full name is Frank Henry Cavendish, Junior .

7) Does Missis Valdez still live at 135 East Seventh Avenue ?

# COMMAS (medium)

The main function of a **comma** (,) is to create a small separation between words, phrases, or clauses. A comma also indicates where a small pause should occur when reading the sentence. The placement of a comma can have a significant impact on the meaning of a sentence. For example, compare "Meet Olivia, Ross, Allie, Dale, and Mr. Reed" (which gives the first names of four people and the last name of another person) with "Meet Olivia Ross, Allie Dale, and Mr. Reed" (which gives the full names of two people and the last name of another person). Commas are used in the following ways:

- Commas separate items in a **series**. Example: Buy paper, pencils, and erasers. Note: The last comma (which comes before **and**), referred to as the **Oxford comma**, is considered optional by some, but helps to avoid confusion in certain cases (which is why many grammar references **recommend** using the Oxford comma). If a list ends with **etc.**, place a comma before it (and after it if **etc.** does not end the sentence). Example: Altitude, turbulence, cabin pressure, etc., factor into the calculation.

- A comma separates two **independent clauses** (which are complete thoughts that would each be complete sentences by themselves) joined by a **coordinating conjunction** (**and**, **or**, **but**, **nor**, **for**, **yet**, or **so**). Example: I would like to discuss this further, but we will be late to class if we don't leave soon. Exception: For short clauses, the comma may be omitted if it does not cause confusion. Note: If a coordinating conjunction joins words or groups of words that are not each complete thoughts, do **not** use a comma (as in "I went to the bowling alley and the tennis court"). This includes the case where two verbs share the same subject (for example, in "We washed the dishes and mopped the floor," the subject **We** applies to the verbs **washed** and **mopped**), though a comma is necessary when omitting the comma may cause confusion (as in "The boy saw the man who walked through the door, and hid," where inserting the comma shows that it was the boy who hid and not the man).

- When a **dependent clause** (it may help to review **subordinating conjunctions**) is placed **before** a main clause, a comma separates the clauses. Example: If it rains this afternoon, wait at school. When a dependent clause comes **after** a main clause, a comma is **not** used if (as is often the case) the dependent clause is essential to the basic meaning of the sentence (as in "Wait at school if it rains this afternoon"); however, if the dependent clause is **not** essential to the basic meaning of the sentence, then a comma **is** used (as in "I will go to the library now, if anybody cares").

- Commas separate a **group of words** (or sometimes a single word) from the rest of a sentence when those words are **not** essential to the basic meaning of the sentence. Example: Our veggie sandwich, which comes with a side of carrots, is on sale this week. (If the separated words are removed, the rest of the sentence conveys the same basic meaning: "Our veggie sandwich is on sale this week.") However, do **not** use commas to separate a group of words that are essential to the basic meaning of a sentence. For example, in "Foods such as chips and ice cream should be avoided while you are training," the words "such as chips and ice cream" are essential; if they are removed, the rest of the sentence conveys a much different meaning: "Foods should be avoided while you are training."

- A comma often separates **introductory words** or phrases. Example: To my knowledge, this has never been done before. Second example: Cupping his hands around his mouth, he shouted instructions to the new recruits. Exceptions: A comma may be optional for an **adverbial phrase**, which functions like an adverb, if omitting the comma does not cause confusion (especially if the phrase is short). For example, a comma after **night** is optional in "At night we will clean the garage," whereas "While eating, Jim received a call from work" needs a comma (otherwise, the sentence begins "While eating Jim," which sounds confusing at first). Do **not** include a comma when an introductory phrase comes **immediately before the verb** that it modifies (as in "In front of the museum stood a statue of the town's founder," where the phrase "in front of the museum" modifies the verb **stood**).

- Commas separate **people** when they are **directly addressed**. Example: Dad, where are you?

- Commas separate **people**, **book titles**, etc., when there is **no** ambiguity about the person or object being referred to. Example: The winner of this year's poetry contest, Connie Miller, will recite one of her poems tonight. (Connie Miller and the winner of this year's contest are the same person, so there is no ambiguity.) In contrast, commas are **not** used when there **would be** ambiguity. For example, in "I received a letter from my friend Julie last night," no commas are used because the speaker has more than just one friend (so **Julie** is considered essential information).

- When multiple adjectives come before the same noun, a comma separates two **adjectives** that belong to the **same category** (recall the section entitled, "Order of Adjectives"), or if the order of the adjectives could be reversed. Example: This is our lazy, irritable cat. The adjectives **lazy** and **irritable** are both opinions; we could alternatively write "irritable, lazy cat." In contrast, a comma is **not** used when one of the adjectives and the noun together form a single unit, or if the order of the adjectives is **not** reversible. For example, there is **no** comma in "cheap plastic containers" because it would not sound correct to write "plastic cheap containers" (**cheap** is an opinion and **plastic** is a material).

- Commas separate **yes** or **no** when they introduce an explanation. Example: Yes, I did my chores this morning.

- Commas separate **interjections** that convey milder emotions (whereas exclamation marks are used to convey stronger emotions). Example: Er, what are you waiting for?

- Commas separate **quotations** if the text within the quotes is a complete sentence and if the quote is **not** introduced by a conjunction. Example: "I wonder," she said, "what lies beyond those mountains." In contrast, **no** comma is used if a quote is introduced by a **conjunction** or if the text within the quotes is **not** a complete sentence. Example: Quit telling everyone that "the sky is falling" (here, **that** functions as a subordinating conjunction). Second example: She called you a "creative genius."

- A comma is used when a person's **name** is **inverted** such that the last name comes first. Compare Jane Doe with Doe, Jane.

- A comma separates a **degree** from a name (like Bryn Myers, M.D.). A comma is **not** needed before **Jr.** or **Sr.** (like Deon Smith Jr.), unless the last name comes first (like Smith, Deon, Jr.).

- A comma separates the year when a **date** is expressed as month-day-year (like August 27, 2016). **No** comma is used when a date is expressed as month-year (like April 2023), season-year (like spring 1996), or day-year (like Christmas 2025).

- Commas separate a **state** or **country** from a city. Example: We plan to visit Eureka Springs, Arkansas, next summer.
- Commas separate the **digits** of numbers of 1,000 or more. Examples: 4,312 and 16,572,384. Exceptions: Street addresses do not use commas (like 12183 Sycamore Ave.), years only use a comma if they have more than four digits (compare 2014 AD with 15,000 BC), and scientific measurements often only use a comma if the value is 10,000 or greater.

**Directions:** Add commas where needed to correct the punctuation.

1) Yes your uncle was born in Miami Florida on September 16 1984.

2) We have tickets to tonight's play and it begins in less than an hour.

3) To her surprise the dishes bowls and cups had been washed and dried.

4) The baby looked at the familiar woman who approached and clapped.

5) Ready or not we will be leaving in an hour to pick up Alan Pratt Sr.

6) Do you Charles know where Leonard was on Friday May 7 2021?

7) Since Amy must be hungry offer her some angel food cake and punch.

8) Her suggestion which proved to be helpful was to find a new tutor.

9) For the second time any medicine that has expired should be discarded.

10) A large brown bear weighs 1500 lbs. which is heavier than a golf cart.

11) Kim Park Ph.D. is a knowledgeable experienced professor of physics.

12) Our boss wants an inventory of nails bolts nuts etc. by next week.

13) The boy said "Mom wants to know where you are Dad."

14) Grandma my coach called me a "quick learner" during practice.

15) She claimed to have been cleaning all day yet the house was messy.

16) Vacuum mop the floors and do the laundry when you get home.

17) When the printer runs out of ink replace the toner cartridge.

18) Hannah Leslie and I played miniature golf and went swimming.

19) Freezing from the snow they lit the fireplace as soon as they entered.

20) Trailing behind them was the mayor Howard Madison III.

21) Well we could visit on May 23 2023 July 9 2023 or March 18 2024.

22) "The movie we saw" he said "was surprisingly charming and witty."

23) Their only son Bart discovered fossils dated 8000 BC and 24000 BC.

24) My cousin Erica was born in Tulsa OK. She is my favorite cousin.

25) Ah that first sip is quite refreshing after a few hours of hard work.

26) With his main competitor out of the race he started to relax a little.

27) The man with the long hair and beard came here from Tokyo Japan.

28) Put your stinky sweaty socks in the hamper not on the couch.

29) My brother left his brown teddy bear on the dining table I think.

30) The child pulling the wagon is the daughter of Marcus Watts M.D.

31) Tying her hair in a pony tail she said "I'm ready to play."

32) His only book *Mayflower* was published on Thanksgiving 1978.

33) Her book *Not Real* was published on April 14 2021. It was her best.

34) Shannon Theresa and I will be in the same class next year I hope.

35) Delighted that the package had arrived she raced down the stairs.

36) With her face covered in chocolate she claimed "I didn't eat them."

37) Mom did Dad really say that "taxes are the cruelest thing ever"?

38) That tractor though it is rusty and dented still gets the job done.

# COLON VS. SEMICOLON (medium)

The main function of a **semicolon** (;) is to join two **independent clauses** (which are complete thoughts that would each be complete sentences by themselves) that are **logically connected**. Following are ways that semicolons should and shouldn't be used.

- A semicolon can join two independent clauses that are logically connected without using a conjunction. Example: My ankle is sore; it was injured during the game.

- If a **conjunctive adverb** (like however, therefore, thus, hence, or besides) joins two independent clauses that are logically connected, a semicolon comes before the adverb and a comma typically follows the adverb if it has multiple syllables (though the comma may be omitted if the sentence seems to be effective without it). Example: The streets are flooded from the rain; therefore, school will be canceled today.

- If a **transitional expression** (like "that is" or "for example") joins two independent clauses that are logically connected, a semicolon comes before the expression and a comma follows it. Example: Electric current takes the path of least resistance; that is, more electrons travel through the smaller resistance each second.

- If a **coordinating conjunction** is used to join two independent clauses, a **comma** usually comes before the conjunction. However, a semicolon may be used instead of a comma to create a stronger sense of separation between the clauses or if the semicolon helps make the sentence structure clear (which may be the case if the second clause uses a pair of commas to separate a group of words). Note: If neither of these two cases applies, either use a comma instead of a semicolon, or use a semicolon without including the conjunction. Example: The politician was not in favor of the proposal; but insistence from other members of his party, along with implications made by lobbyists, persuaded him to vote for it.

- When items are listed in a **series**, the items are usually separated by **commas**. However, semicolons may be used instead of commas if the semicolons help make the sentence structure clear (which may be the case if the items themselves include commas). Example: She went to Hawaii with Liz, Sadie, and Nina; Miami with Sadie, Nina, and Carly; and Denver with Liz, Carly, and Zoe.

- **Don't** capitalize the first word that follows the semicolon (unless that word happens to be a proper noun or a proper adjective).

- **Don't** use a semicolon if the two clauses do **not** share a logical connection. For example, "The dog is chasing its tail" and "It is raining today" do **not** share any logical connection.

- **Don't** use a semicolon if either clause is **not** a complete thought (meaning that the clause would not be a complete sentence by itself). For example, although "My cat is taking a nap" is a complete thought, "so sleepy" is **not** a complete thought.

The main function of a **colon** (:) is to introduce the information that follows it. The colon is a punctuation mark that means "as follows." Following are ways that colons should and shouldn't be used.

- A colon comes before a **list** of items if the text that comes before the colon is a complete thought (meaning that it would form a complete sentence by itself). Such a list sometimes follows introductory words (like "as follows" or "the following"), but sometimes it doesn't. Example: Elements are composed of three kinds of particles: protons, neutrons, and electrons.

- The text after a colon may **explain** or **expand** upon information in an independent clause that comes before the colon. A complete thought comes before the colon, but not necessarily after the colon (whereas for a semicolon, a complete thought comes before and after). Example: Take the medicine as follows: one pill each morning after breakfast.

- The text after a colon may ask a **direct question** if it is introduced by the independent clause that comes before the colon. Example: Consider this question: Is the bottle half full or half empty?

- When a **quotation** is introduced, it is usually set off by **commas**. A colon may be used (especially after introductory words like "as follows" or "the following," or if a lengthy excerpt is quoted) to introduce a quotation, but it comes across as more formal (and usually isn't used with **said**, **replied**, and similar verbs). Example: The valedictorian concluded her speech with the following suggestion: "Let's make the most of it."

- In the case of **dialog** where each speaker has its own paragraph (as in a **play**), a colon may be used after each speaker. Example:
    Harley: What did you eat for lunch today?
    Miguel: Pasta with roasted vegetables. And you?

- A colon separates a **subtitle** from a title. Example: We just finished streaming *Star Trek*: *The Next Generation*.

- A colon separates pairs of **digits** when telling time, indicating ratios, citing *Bible* verses, or citing volume and page numbers. Example: At 3:15 p.m., the ratio of apples to oranges was 5:4.

- A colon is used after addressing a person in a letter or formal communication. Example: Dear Dr. Lopez:

- Only **capitalize** the first word that follows the colon if the colon introduces more than one complete sentence, a direct question follows the colon, a quotation (that is a complete thought) follows the colon, writing dialog like that of a play, the colon introduces the subtitle of a title, or the word following the colon happens to be a proper noun or a proper adjective. Otherwise, **don't** capitalize the first word that follows the colon (such as when a list of items follows the colon, when an incomplete thought follows the colon, or when the text following the colon would form a single complete sentence that isn't a quotation or a direct question).

- **Don't** use a colon if the text before the colon would **not** form a complete thought. For example, "We are running out of paper towels, toilet paper, and napkins" does not use a colon because "We are running out of" is **not** a complete thought.

**Directions**: Add semicolons, colons, or commas where needed to correct the punctuation.

1) She painted the picture using three colors blue black and yellow.

2) I need to change my tie I spilled coffee on this one.

3) Let's go to the library it's a quiet place to study.

4) He always hides his snack in the same place a box under his bed.

5) The omelet was cooked to perfection fluffy with melted cheese.

6) It is already 745 a.m. you are running late for school.

7) The old saying proved to be true "What goes around comes around."

8) My uncle has two left feet that is he is a clumsy dancer.

9) These are thoughts I strive to live by Be kind. Be positive. Be happy.

10) Let me ask you this If you could have a superpower what would it be?

11) Has your sister read *Pinkalicious Tickled Pink* by Victoria Kann?

12) Victor is recovering from a hamstring injury otherwise he would be running in the marathon.

13) My brother eats an unusual combination of foods at the same time for a snack celery and rice cakes.

14) I used the internet to take virtual tours of the following places Moscow Russia England Paris France Italy and Cairo Egypt.

15) Kyle is waiting for his mother to pick him up he has been waiting here since 315 p.m.

16) He wrote a story entirely out of clichés for example it begins with the following line "Once upon a time it was a dark and stormy night."

17) We watched *Spider-Man No Way Home* we thought that the movie was good but we liked *Spider-Man Homecoming* better.

18) Follow these directions Preheat the oven to 375 degrees. Place the pizza on a cookie sheet. Cook for 18 to 21 minutes.

19) That goat will eat almost anything for instance one time when I was cleaning his pen he started to chew my pant leg.

20) I earned the following grades this semester B's in language arts physical science and social studies A's in algebra computer science and physical education and C's in graphic arts and college prep.

21) The car is low on gas therefore we will need to stop at the gas station on the way home.

22) Maybe Andrew would sign up for summer camp besides he had been wanting to learn how to swim.

23) The highest US population totals in 2020 were 8804190 in New York NY 3898747 in Los Angeles CA 2746388 in Chicago IL 2304580 in Houston TX and 1608139 in Phoenix AZ.

# APOSTROPHES (medium)

An **apostrophe** (') almost always signifies either **contraction** (meaning that one or more letters has been omitted) or **possession** (which is a sense of belonging). It is usually **incorrect** to use an apostrophe to form a **plural**, though a few rare exceptions are mentioned below.

- When a phrase is shortened by removing one or more letters and merging the words together, this process is called **contraction** and the resulting word is also called a **contraction**. Examples: I'm (short for "I am"), can't (short for "can not"). Note: Contraction can also occur when a single word is shortened (as in gov't, which is short for "government").

- The **possessive** case of a noun uses an apostrophe to indicate a sense of belonging. Recall the rules from the section entitled "Possessive" from earlier in this book (pages 14–15 in the paperback edition). Examples: cat's tail, Bob's tie, women's clothing, boss's desk, Tess's hair, Mars's orbit, Moses' mother, Archimedes' principle, boys' lockers, group's leader, class's teacher, the Jones' boat. Exception: **Possessive pronouns** (ours, yours, his, hers, its, theirs) do **not** use an apostrophe (as in "The boy waved his hand").

- Most **plurals** do **not** use an apostrophe. (Recall the section entitled "Plurals" from earlier in this book). Examples: dogs, trees, peaches. The exceptions to this rule are rare. One example is when a plural of a single lowercase letter of the alphabet is needed (as in "There are three a's in the word *banana*"). Another example is when an abbreviation has multiple periods (as in "She is one of the rare people to have earned two Ph.D.'s"); when an abbreviation has a single period, the **s** often goes before the period (as in "Read Vols.

3-4 over the summer"). When abbreviations don't have periods, an apostrophe is usually unnecessary (as in "Those are my DVDs"). It is usually unnecessary to use an apostrophe for the plural of a number (as in "I earned two 95s in my history class last week").

**Directions:** Add apostrophes where needed to correct the punctuation.

1) The students didnt know when Abraham Lincolns birthday was.

2) Well visit Nguyens mothers neighbors on the way back.

3) That shirts pattern is dull. Of all the shirts, whyd he buy that one?

4) Hes upset that Cassies new puppy doesnt seem to like him.

5) Fixing Dads computer shouldnt take long. Ill be there soon.

6) We havent done much yet. Youve done much more than we have.

7) His friends sister said, "These arent my slippers. Theyre hers."

8) Shed packed the childrens clothes days before the vacation began.

9) Chriss clock wasnt working this morning. Thats why hes late today.

10) Were driving past the Klines house now. They are nice neighbors.

11) Dont worry; there are three M.D.s in this room.

12) You know that youre not allowed in the gym without your gym shoes.

13) Not one of the librarys books had the information that he wanted.

14) Lets choose the teams. The referee will now hide both teams tokens.

15) Ill stay at Nicholas house this weekend. His parents invited me.

16) I still have time to dot my is and cross my ts before I turn it in.

17) Its surprising that the company lost all of its contracts this year.

18) Whos responsible for washing the skyscrapers windows?

# CONTRACTIONS (easy)

The process of shortening words or phrases by removing letters is called **contraction**. A word that is formed this way is also called a **contraction**. It is customary to avoid contractions in formal writing. Contractions are more common in quotes when characters are speaking in fiction.

- Many contractions form by merging two words together. Examples: **doesn't** stands for **does not**; **he'll** stands for **he will**.

- Few contractions shorten a single word. Example: **'tween** is an old poetic contraction of **between**.

**Directions:** Write out what each contraction is short for.

1) hadn't

2) you'll

3) she's

4) won't

5) they're

6) let's

7) I'm

8) could've

9) 'tis

10) we'd

11) y'all

12) ma'am

13) who've

14) 'til

15) 'twas

16) int'l

# QUOTATION MARKS (medium)

When a writer wants to show the exact words that a person (which may be a real person or a fictional character in a story) said (or wrote), these words appear in a pair of **quotation marks**. There are two kinds of quotation marks:

- **Double quotation marks** are standard. Example: She said, "The air in my bicycle tire is getting low."

- **Single quotation marks** are used (in the United States) when one quotation appears within another quotation. Example: Tyrone said, "I heard that Leo said, 'Calculus is awesome.' Did he really?"

The rules below indicate when to (or not to) use quotation marks.

- Use quotation marks for a **direct quotation**, meaning that the words enclosed in quotation marks are exactly what the speaker said. Example: James said, "Lou's story doesn't seem very likely."

- Do **not** use quotation marks for an **indirect quotation**, meaning that the words are not exactly what the speaker says. Example: James said that Lou's story seemed unlikely.

- Quotation marks are used for the **titles of short works**, whereas italics are used for the titles of long works. Examples of short works include stories, articles, chapters, poems, and songs. Examples of long works include books and movies. Example: I just read "A Hunger Artist" in *Franz Kafka: The Complete Stories*.

- A word or expression may be enclosed in quotation marks to indicate that its usage is **nonstandard, specialized, skeptical, ironic, sarcastic, derisive, or intentionally incorrect**. (An alternative is to use italics.) Example: These so-called "healthy" snacks are loaded with sugar.

- If a word (or expression) is used to refer to the **word itself**, some writers enclose the word in quotation marks (while other writers use italics instead). Example: What does the word "acumen" mean?

When using quotation marks, follow these rules:

- When a **comma** or **period** comes at the end of a quotation, it comes **before** the end quotation mark. Example: "Grandma," he said, "bakes the best apple pies."

- When a **colon** or **semicolon** comes at the end of a quotation, it comes **after** the end quotation mark. Example: Following are synonyms for the word "pressure": stress, strain, and tension. Second example: Read the play "Twelve Angry Men"; we will hold an audition for parts next week.

- When a **question mark** or **exclamation mark** comes at the end of a quotation, it can come before or after the end quotation mark depending on the situation. It comes before the end quotation mark if the quotation itself is a question or exclamation; otherwise, it comes after the end quotation mark. Example: Who said, "I love anchovies on my pizza"? (The quotation itself is **not** a question, so the question mark goes **outside**.) Second example: He asked, "Do you have plans for the weekend?" (The quotation itself **is** a question, so the question mark goes **inside**.)

- Capitalize the first letter of the first word of a **quotation** if the text within the quotes is a complete sentence, like "It's supposed to rain today," but not otherwise, like "a diamond in the rough."

- If an **apostrophe** comes at the end of a word, the apostrophe always comes **before** another punctuation mark (whereas **single quotation marks** follow the rules listed previously). Example with an apostrophe: The house on the corner is the McIlroys'. Example with single quotation marks: Nancy said, "Abigail called the movie an 'emotional roller coaster.'"

- When two people are speaking, start a new paragraph to indicate that the speaker has changed. In the example below, Juan speaks in the third paragraph and Gabriel speaks in the last paragraph.

    "That exam was harder than I had expected," said Juan.

    "Same here," said Gabriel. "I wish I had studied more."

    "We should form a study group before the next exam."

    "That's a good idea."

- If the same speaker talks for two or more paragraphs (or if a quoted excerpt has two or more paragraphs), each paragraph begins with quotation marks, but only the last paragraph of the multi-paragraph quotation ends with quotation marks. Note how the first paragraph below does **not** have an end quotation mark because the mother continues speaking in the next paragraph.

    "I'll be home before you know it," Mom said. "The trip is only for three days. You'll be busy while I'm away. Time will pass quickly. I'll call you every night.

    "Remember to do your chores before I return. Help your father watch your brother. I love you. Goodbye."

**Directions:** Add quotation marks, capitalize words, and add italics (or underline if writing by hand) where needed to correct the punctuation.

1) Ms. Hathaway said, the final exam counts for ten percent of the final grade and covers material from throughout the semester.

2) The refund policy states, merchandise may be returned for a refund or exchange within 30 days with a receipt of purchase.

3) Professor, asked Simon, what does the word doohickey mean? Is that a particular kind of device?

4) We recently read the poem Jabberwocky by Lewis Carroll in A Treasury of Favorite Poems.

5) The booklet states, the wand will glow for up to eight hours. To summarize the rest, it says that we should avoid contact with skin.

6) We are glad that all of you came, said the host, to help us celebrate the graduation of our twin sons, Jerry and Jose.

7) Naomi wrote a short story called Looking without Seeing; it is much different from her first short story, Seemingly Endless.

8) The child kept repeating the words dry mouth until her mother handed her a bottle of juice.

9) Kids screamed that a spider was in the house. The father yelled, stop shouting! When it was quiet, the father escorted the spider outside.

10) My mom only likes two songs better than Selena Gomez's Rare: Shake it Off by Taylor Swift and Better Be Good to Me by Tina Turner.

11) The teacher asked, what are the last four words of The Star-Spangled Banner? Is the answer home of the brave?

12) Quit singing the song Grandma Got Run Over by a Reindeer! That song is starting to get on my nerves.

13) Did you see the helicopter on the roof of the building? she asked. That helicopter is Mr. Williams'.

14) We're trying to see, he said, how many words we can form using letters in the word language.

15) Becca said, can I eat the soup now? I'm starving.

    Her mother replied, it's very hot. Wait for it to cool down.

    Please let me try. I'll be careful.

    Okay. But remember that I warned you.

# HYPHENS (easy)

A **hyphen** (-) is a short horizontal line that joins words (or numbers) together, or which divides a word that is too long to fit at the end of a line in text that is typed. (Don't confuse a hyphen with a dash, which is a longer horizontal line that serves a different purpose.)

- Hyphens are used to form **phrasal adjectives** that come immediately before a noun. Example: one-way street.

- Some standard **compound words** use hyphens. Example: self-esteem.

- A writer may come across a rare situation where a hyphen may help the reader to avoid possible confusion; in such a case, the hyphen serves to help **clarify** the meaning. For example, a hyphen may be inserted in **re-create** if the writer is using the word to mean "to create again," in order to avoid confusion with the unhyphenated **recreate** (meaning "to put fresh life into"). Cases like this are rare.

- A hyphen is used to attach a **prefix** to a proper noun (or adjective), an acronym, or years. Examples: non-English speaking, mid-1990s.

- A hyphen is used when **writing out numbers**. For example, when 463 is written out, a hyphen is used: four hundred sixty-three.

- Many style guides recommend using an **en dash** (which is longer than a hyphen) instead of a hyphen for **number ranges**, yet it is not uncommon to see a **hyphen** used instead (especially, when the writing is not a formal publication). Compare 36–39 with 36-39.

- Hyphens are used to separate groups of digits in **non-inclusive numbers**, meaning that the numbers **don't** represent a range. For example, the phone number 555-1212 uses a hyphen, whereas the inclusive range 17–21 (meaning 17 thru 21) uses an en dash.

- A speaker may use hyphens to separate letters when spelling out words. Example: "The name of my birth city," he said, "is spelled J-u-n-e-a-u. It is the capital of Alaska."

- In **typewritten works,** a hyphen is used to avoid creating large gaps of white space between words (if the paragraph is justified full) or to avoid creating a large gap of white space at the end of a line (if the paragraph is ragged right, meaning that the lines are aligned only at the left) when a word is too long to fit at the end of a line. In this case, a hyphen divides a word into two parts where a syllable ends. For example, in the paperback edition of this work-book, the word **workbook** was hyphenated in this manner; the first syllable (**work**) appears at the end of one line along with the hyphen, and the second syllable (**book**) appears at the beginning of the next line. Here, the hyphen functions to tell the reader that the word continues onto the next line of the paragraph.

**Directions:** Add hyphens where needed to correct the punctuation.

1) Nathan's sister in law is friends with Collin's daughter in law.

2) One student answered forty eight out of fifty questions correctly.

3) Please give this yo yo to the boy wearing the blue T shirt.

4) Your photo will look nicer if you apply the red eye filter.

5) The phone number 555 1212 is used in movies and television shows.

6) It was unlike any other fourteenth century painting she had seen.

7) Three fourths of the patients never had an X ray taken before.

8) His parents signed him up for a top notch golf academy.

9) "My name is Marcous," the boy said. "It's spelled M a r c o u s."

10) The combination to the locker is 18 31 15.

# COMPOUND WORDS (easy)

A **compound** is a word that is formed from shorter words.

- An **open compound** has two (or more) words separated by a space. Examples: middle school, coffee table.
- A **closed compound** has two (or more) words joined together without a space. Examples: flashlight, alongside.
- A **hyphenated compound** has two (or more) words joined by hyphens. Examples: close-up, merry-go-round.

**Directions:** Write out the compound that the given words form.

1) tea + cup

2) pet + food

3) one + sided

4) health + care

5) pencil + cup

6) part + time

7) over + night

8) leap + year

9) runner + up

10) guard + rail

11) sea + salt

12) high + rise

13) four + wheel + drive

14) what + so + ever

15) foot + ball + stadium

16) tri + state + area

# PHRASAL ADJECTIVES (medium)

A **phrasal adjective** is a group of words that form a single thought that modifies a noun. The rules below help to determine whether or not to hyphenate a phrasal adjective.

- If a phrasal adjective comes **before** the noun it modifies, it should be hyphenated (unless the phrasal adjective begins with **very** or an **ly** adverb). Example: The book has black-and-white illustrations.

- If a phrasal adjective begins with **very** or an **ly** adverb, it should **not** be hyphenated. Example: I had a very nice weekend. Second example: They are a happily married couple.

- If a phrasal adjective comes **after** a noun, hyphenation is usually **not** necessary. Example: The illustrations are black and white. (Contrast this with the example from the first bullet point.)

- If two adjectives modify the same noun, **only** hyphenate them if together they form a **single thought** that modifies the noun. Example: Hand me the fine-toothed comb. If instead they function as two **separate** adjectives, do **not** hyphenate them; also, follow the rule for the order of adjectives (as in "an expensive pearl necklace") and use a comma if their order may be reversed (as in "a safe, quiet community").

**Directions**: Add hyphens or commas where they are needed. (Beware that some of these sentences may be fine just as they are.)

1) The spacious closet included a full length mirror.

2) Biographies can be found in the second to last aisle.

3) My brother finished the race second to last.

82

4) The forecast calls for partly cloudy skies over the weekend.

5) I am twenty nine years old. Have you met my three year old son?

6) Stephanie proved to be a very sweet girl.

7) All we have left is a half eaten sandwich.

8) The ceiling is twelve feet high. I need my eight foot ladder.

9) We really like the hands free faucet in the bathroom.

10) This is the delightful charming neighbor I was telling you about.

11) The manager was fond of the new employee's can do attitude.

12) It's the twenty first century, yet he has a horse drawn carriage.

13) Nobody will believe his story about the little green men.

14) Here is an up to date list of dentists in our state.

15) Our records are always up to date.

16) They call it a five star neighborhood, but I would give it three stars.

17) It was a once in a lifetime opportunity.

# WORD DIVISION (challenge)

When a word does not fit at the end of a line of typewritten text, if moving the word onto the next line creates significant undesirable white space, a hyphen may be used to divide the word across the lines. The rule is to **divide the word between syllables**. In the paperback edition of this workbook, the word **edition** is hyphenated, with a break between the first two syllables (**edi-**) and the last syllable (**tion**). The following rules help to divide a word at the end of a line with a hyphen.

- A word is usually divided into **syllables** based on how the word **sounds** when it is **spoken**. Try sounding the word out. Examples: di-rect, sim-ply, prin-ci-pal, in-for-ma-tion.

- A **closed syllable** ends with a consonant and often has a short vowel sound. Examples (with the closed syllable underlined): **han**-dle, **mag**-**net**, bro-**ken**. When a two-syllable word begins with a closed syllable, the word usually divides between two consonants (like **pic**-ture).

- An **open syllable** ends with a vowel and often has a long vowel sound when it begins a two-syllable word. Examples (with the open syllable underlined): **do**-nate, **ty**-rant, **tro**-**phy**, fore-**go**. When a two-syllable word begins with an open syllable, the word usually divides after a vowel (like **clo**-sure).

- When a syllable ends with **le**, the word usually divides before the consonant that comes before **le**. Examples (with the **le** syllable underlined): tan-**gle**, sta-**ple**.

- Some syllables end with a silent **e** that often signals a long vowel sound. Examples (with the silent **e** syllable underlined): **fore**-cast, ex-**cite**, **use**-ful.

- Multiple letters may create a single vowel sound (like the **ow** in **pow**-er-ful or in **snow**-ball, or like the **eau** in **beau**-ti-ful), but sometimes consecutive vowels create separate vowel sounds (like the **ie** in **pli**-**ers** or the **eo** in **ge**-**og**-ra-phy).

- Beware that a few words actually divide differently when used as a **noun** than when used as a **verb**. For example, when **present** is used as a noun or adjective, it divides as pres-ent (where the first syllable has a short **e** and stress is placed on the first syllable), but when **present** is used as a verb, it divides as pre-sent (where the first syllable has a long e and stress is placed on the last syllable).

- **One-syllable** words (like **strained**) should **not** be hyphenated. **One-letter divisions** are **not** permitted (so words like **evolve**, which has syllables **e**+**volve**, should **not** be hyphenated).

- When a word with three or more syllables includes a **one-letter syllable**, it is better to divide the word after the one-letter syllable than before it. For example, **dialog** (which has syllables di+a+log) should be divided as dia-log (not as di-alog).

- When a word has three or more syllables, there are often **preferred breaking** points determined by prefixes or roots. For example, **understood** should be divided as under-stood (not un-derstood). However, beware that **not** all words divide at their prefixes, roots, or suffixes. For example, while **remain** divides as re-main, **remedy** divides as rem-edy (even though the prefix is **re**).

- Participles and gerunds ending with **ing** divide at the **ing** unless the **ing** is part of a closed syllable (**ing** is usually part of a closed syllable when it follows a double letter that doesn't break up a root). Examples (with the **ing** syllable underlined): mak-**ing**, drum-**ming**, hurt-**ing**. Note: The **ing** usually doesn't break up the root (hurt-**ing** instead of hur-ting and fall-**ing** instead of fal-ling).

- Avoid dividing website URLs and email addresses. If it must be broken, don't use a hyphen (because some website URLs actually include hyphens in them). If a URL or email address includes a hyphen, don't break it at the hyphen (since the reader may not realize that the hyphen is necessary if that is done).
- When in doubt, a good **dictionary** shows the preferred word divisions. Many word processors offer **automatic hyphenation**.

**Directions:** Where may each word be hyphenated (if at all)?

1) fraction

2) decent

3) blanket

4) zipper

5) social

6) trained

7) humble

8) eyebrow

9) battle

10) surgeon

11) precise

12) figure

13) ocean

14) basement

15) farming

16) winning

17) trifle

18) tribute

19) joyous

20) tailor

21) pleasant

22) reaction

23) alternate

24) loneliness

25) serious

26) opposite

27) concerning

28) intertwine

29) magazine

30) temperature

31) facilitate

32) unbelievable

# DASHES (easy)

A **dash** (– or —) is longer than a hyphen (-) and is used differently than a hyphen. There are two kinds of dashes: an **en dash** (–) and an **em dash** (—). The **en dash** (–) is shorter than an **em dash** (—). They are so named because an **en dash** (–) is about as wide as an uppercase "N" and an **em dash** (—) is about as wide as an uppercase "M."

- Traditionally, the **en dash** (–) is used for **number ranges**. Example: Read pages 58–91. (Note: It is not uncommon, especially in informal writing, to see a **hyphen** instead: 58-91. For a typeface where the **en dash** seems excessively long for this and the **hyphen** seems too short, you can create something in between: 58-91.)

- Traditionally, the **em dash** (—) is used to **interrupt the flow of writing** to explain or expand upon the information. As a separator, a dash is less formal than a colon, not a side note like parentheses, and more abrupt than a comma. No spaces surround an **em dash**—like this. Do **not** put a comma or semicolon before an **em dash**; however, a question mark or exclamation mark **may** come before an **em dash**. Example: The Carrington's have two daughters—ages eight and eleven. Second example: He reached into the jewelry box and pulled out a locket—inside it was a photo of Regina's grandmother—and handed it to Regina. Third example: The team captain—that's me!—will make that decision.

- In the age of eBooks, blogs, websites, and other digital forms, text is often displayed in a reflowable format, meaning that it is not possible to predict which words will fill the screen (since readers use different screen sizes, font sizes, etc.). Some of these digital works (including popular Kindle readers) have inherent challenges with formatting the dash. As a result, in digital works, it is becoming increasingly common to see **en dashes** (–) used instead of **em dashes** (—). For this usage, a space surrounds each **en dash** (whereas **no** spaces surround an **em dash**) – like this.

**Directions:** Insert dashes where needed to correct the punctuation.

1) When she went to the museum with her friends last week, the strangest thing happened just a minute, I need to take this phone call.

2) Two of our cats the striped one and the gray one woke me up last night because they had gotten locked in my room.

3) I still need to grab my things have you seen my passport? before we drive to the airport.

4) "Let's see," he said. "You owe me five no, it's actually seven dollars for your supplies."

5) "The girl reading the newspaper" she lowered her voice to a whisper "knows everyone at the school. You should ask her."

6) We're cycling past the dump ew, that odor is disgusting! right now on our way to the theater.

# PARENTHESES (easy)

**Parentheses** () set aside information that is non-essential for understanding the sentence itself, but which may help or interest the reader. Example: Sir Isaac Newton (1642-1727) revolutionized our understanding of physics. Second example: I brought my mom's cookies to the living room (after sneaking one into my mouth). The rules below indicate how parentheses combine with other punctuation marks.

- If parentheses are used in **part** of a sentence and the closing parentheses mark comes at the end of the sentence, a **period** comes **after** the closing **parentheses** mark (first example); if instead parentheses enclose an **entire sentence**, a **period** comes **before** the closing **parentheses** mark (second example). Example: Calvin always offered to help (but only to seem polite). Second example: I painted one of those pictures. (You'll never guess which one.)

- If a **question mark**, **exclamation mark**, or **quotation mark** appears next to a closing parentheses mark, it comes **before** the closing **parentheses** mark if it is **part of the parenthetical comment** (first example) and **after** the closing **parentheses** otherwise (second example). Example: I can't believe Sandy turned thirteen today (where does the time fly?). Second example: Would you please bring some paper towels (if there are any left)?

- A **comma** or **semicolon** should **not** be next to an **opening parentheses** mark, except when parentheses are used to enumerate the items in a list like this: (a) Mercury, (b) Venus, and (c) earth. A **comma** or **semicolon** should **not** come before a closing **parentheses** mark, but they may come after a closing parentheses mark. Example: After we ate pasta (my specialty), we went for a walk.

**Square brackets** [] may be used in the following ways:

- If one parenthetical comment appears inside of another, place the **inner comment** in brackets. Example: We will now apply the rules for congruent triangles to right triangles. (It may help to review the Pythagorean theorem [Chapter 4]).

- Brackets are used when a writer quotes material and makes a **clarification** or slight **alteration** to what is **quoted**. For example, suppose that a coach said "He played great tonight" during an interview after a game. If a writer quotes this single sentence, the writer may clarify the player's name like this: "He [Bradley] played great tonight." As another example, suppose that a writer quotes only the second part of a compound sentence, and the part that is quoted forms a complete thought, so it needs to be capitalized: "[G]iraffes run surprisingly quick."

**Directions:** Insert the closing parentheses marks and closing brackets.

1) Michelangelo (1475-1564 is famous for his Renaissance artwork.

2) Read about metaphors (pp. 163-178 before our next class.

3) My sister is a huge fan of horror (don't ask me why novels and movies.

4) It sounds like it will be fun (too bad I have to work tomorrow.

5) She doesn't even know that I exist. (Sigh.

6) Paint was peeling (inside and outside, so I hired a handyman.

7) Does anyone know what we're supposed to do (because I don't?

8) You love teaching (don't you? and we have a lecturer position to fill.

9) "The author [Sheena Patel is currently working on her third novel."

10) Her lab was donated by one of our alumni (J.D. Farr [1938–2017.

# ELLIPSIS POINTS (easy)

**Ellipsis points** (. . .) either indicate omitted words or a pause.

- Ellipsis points may indicate that words were **omitted from a quotation** (provided that the omission doesn't alter the meaning). Example: "He taught piano . . . for twenty years."

- Ellipsis points function as suspension points when they indicate a deliberate **pause** or fragmented/interrupted speech. Example: She said, "I . . . I . . . don't know . . . what else to say."

- If the text before ellipsis points forms a complete thought and a new sentence begins after the ellipsis points, a **period** is needed before the ellipsis points (for a total of four dots). Example: "We went to the park. . . . The neighbor's babysitter was there."

- If the first word after ellipsis points does **not** begin a new sentence, **don't** capitalize it. Example: "They decided to . . . forget the matter entirely." If instead the first word after ellipsis points **does** begin a new sentence, **do** capitalize it. Example: "We met in the summer. . . . We haven't seen each other since then."

**Directions**: Use ellipsis points in place of the boxed words.

1) I visited family and friends in Vermont last week.

2) The radio made a loud hum before it stopped working.

3) She ran like the wind and won a bronze medal.

4) The cat chased a lizard and broke a vase.

5) He said during the meeting that it won't matter.

6) We played cards on the porch . It was fun.

# ITALICS (medium)

<u>**Italics**</u> are used for the titles of long works (like books), to add emphasis to a word or phrase, for a foreign term, or when a word or expression is used outside of its usual context. <u>**Underlining**</u> is equivalent to italics. If you write by hand (or use a typewriter), use underlining instead of italics.

- Italics (or underlining) is used for the <u>**titles of long works**</u>, whereas quotation marks are used for the titles of short works. Examples of long works include books, movies, artwork, magazines, newspapers, and ships (including boats, aircraft, and spacecraft). Short works include stories, articles, chapters, poems, and songs. Example: She will read "Sleeping Beauty" from *Classic Bedtime Stories* to her son tonight. Second example: In 1969, *Apollo 11* landed on the moon.

- Italics (or underlining) may be used to add <u>**emphasis**</u> to a word or phrase (when the writing is informal). This can be effective if it is done sparingly. Example: You're sitting in *my* chair.

- Italics (or underlining) may be used for a foreign term (especially, if many readers are not expected to be familiar with it). Example: He said that he only speaks *un peu français*.

- Italics (or underlining) may be applied to a word or expression that is used outside of its usual context. (Sometimes quotation marks are used for this purpose instead.) Example: Your tax *professional* didn't even know the most basic tax laws.

- Italics (or underlining) may be applied when a word (or expression) is used to refer to the <u>**word itself**</u>. (An alternative is to use quotation marks.) Example: Could you please tell me what the word *facetious* means?

**Directions:** Add italics (or underline if writing by hand) and add quotation marks where needed to correct the punctuation.

1) Our teacher asked us to read the chapter called Periodic Properties of the Elements in the book entitled Chemistry: The Central Science.

2) Posted on his wall was an article with the headline Berlin Wall Tumbles from the London Herald newspaper.

3) "This woman is looking for her welpe," said the girl. "From her gestures, I think it means that she lost her puppy."

4) Do you know if the book A Treasury of Favorite Poems includes the poem A Dream Within a Dream by Edgar Allen Poe?

5) Titanic, Pride & Prejudice, and Bridget Jones's Diary are three of my mother's favorite movies.

6) Do you know the distinction between the words predicament, dilemma, and quandary?

7) I read the article Why movies need the big screen in Time magazine (Vol. 192, Nos. 19-20).

8) When the man saw the shiny red sports car pass by, he exclaimed, "Mamma mia! Now that's a fancy ride!"

9) Rembrandt's famous painting The Night Watch (1642) sold for over 70 million dollars in 1998.

10) My little brother loves watching Shaun the Sheep's thirtieth episode from the second season, which is entitled The Big Chase.

11) In 1620, the Mayflower sailed from England to America with over one hundred passengers.

12) Keegan was dancing along to the song No Judgement from the album Heartbreak Weather by Niall Horan.

# SUBJECT VS. PREDICATE (medium)

A sentence has a subject and a predicate.

- The **simple subject** includes only the main noun(s) or pronoun(s) that is doing the action described by the verb(s). Note that the subject is doing the action (whereas a direct object receives the action) of the verb. For example, in "Lee called Mike," the simple subject is **Lee** because Lee does the calling (whereas the direct object is **Mike** because Mike receives the call). Every sentence has a subject (but not all sentences have an object; recall that intransitive verbs don't take a direct object). The **complete subject** includes the simple subject and also includes words that modify the simple subject. For example, consider the sentence "The young child threw the red ball over the fence again." The simple subject is the noun **child** and the complete subject is **The young child**. Note that a sentence can have a **compound subject**, as in "Melanie and Grace went to the movies," where **Melanie and Grace** form the compound subject. **Tip:** The simple subject won't be in a prepositional phrase. For example, consider the sentence "Behind the door, the boy waited patiently." Here, the door is not the simple subject because the door is in a prepositional phrase. The verb is **waited**. To find the simple subject, ask the question "Who waited?" Since the boy waited, **boy** is the simple subject. Note: Although every sentence has both a subject and a predicate, it is possible for the subject to be **implied**. For example, the subject is implied in the one-word sentence "Stop!"

- The **simple predicate** only includes the verb(s) that describes the action or condition of the subject. The **complete predicate** includes the simple predicate and also includes any other words that describe what the subject is doing or what condition the subject is in. For example, consider the sentence "The young child threw the red ball over the fence again." The simple predicate is **threw** and the complete predicate is **threw the red ball over the fence again**. Note that a sentence can have a **compound predicate**, as in "The cat hissed and then scampered away," where the compound predicate includes two verbs—**hissed** and **scampered**.

**Directions:** Identify the simple (or compound) subject and the simple (or compound) predicate in each sentence.

1) Unfortunately, Richard never passed the football to me.

2) On a rainy day, water dripped through a crack in the ceiling.

3) It was quite ridiculous, really.

4) Only a pair of shoes remained in the student's locker.

5) A suit and a tie were the first items on the shopping list.

6) Dr. Sasha Malovic prescribed medicine for my grandfather.

7) The car made several loud noises and shook violently.

8) He slowly and cautiously tiptoed along the corridor.

9) With the exception of Judy, nobody is ready for the tournament.

10) Mr. and Mrs. Hope ate dinner and watched a movie together.

11) Please follow my advice and use common sense.

12) Maria, Nicole, and Riley nearly collided during the basketball game.

13) Out of the fog came a flock of birds.

14) Invite all of your friends to your birthday party.

# COMPLEMENTS (challenge)

A **complement** refers to a word or a group of words which complete (or enhance) the meaning or structure of the predicate. There are five kinds of complements: direct object, object complement, indirect object, predicate adjective, and predicate nominative. (The predicate adjective and predicate nominative are called subject complements.)

- A **direct object** receives the action of a transitive verb. A direct object is usually a noun or a pronoun (but it could also be a clause that functions as a noun). The subject does the action to the object. Example: Maurice drove **Darius** to the store. (The simple subject is **Maurice**, the verb is **drove**, and the direct object is **Darius**.)

- An **object complement** describes, clarifies, or enhances the meaning of a direct object. An object complement is an adjective, noun, or pronoun (or a phrase that functions as one of these). Example: She dyed her hair **red**. (The adjective **red** complements the direct object **hair**.) Second example: Ask my **brother** Travis. (The noun **brother** complements the direct object **Travis**.)

- An **indirect object** comes before a direct object and has an unwritten **to** or **for** implied in its usage. (Note that if the word **to** or **for** is actually written, then it is part of a prepositional phrase, and is **not** an indirect object.) Example: He gave the **dog** a bone. (The noun **dog** is an indirect object because the sentence could be written, "He gave a bone to the dog." In the rewritten sentence that includes the word **to**, the words **to the dog** form a prepositional phrase; in the rewritten sentence, dog is **not** an indirect object. In either case, **bone** is the direct object of the verb **gave** because the bone is what was given.)

- A **predicate adjective** is an adjective that follows a **linking verb** and which modifies the subject. (It may help to review the section entitled "Linking Verbs"; a brief review is given below.) Example: Today's meeting was **brief**. (The adjective **brief** follows the linking verb **was** and describes the subject **meeting**.)

- A **predicate nominative** is a noun or pronoun that follows a **linking verb** and which describes, clarifies, or enhances the meaning of the subject. Example: The girl by the window is my **sister**. (The noun **sister** follows the linking verb **is** and provides a detail about the subject **girl**.)

Recall that a **linking verb** includes forms of the verb **to be** (like **am**, **is**, **are**, **was**, and **were**), the verbs **seem** and **become**, and some other verbs (like **look**, **feel**, **taste**, **grow**, and **stay**) that are sometimes linking verbs (they are when they are interchangeable with a form of **to be**; for example, in "I feel sad," **feel** is a linking verb because we can write "I am sad," but in "I feel slime," feel is **not** a linking verb because "I am slime" doesn't preserve the meaning of the original sentence).

In highly formal English, forms of the verb **to be** take a subject instead of an object. That is, it is historically accurate to say expressions like "It is I" instead of "It is me." (This rule derives from other languages like Latin.) However, in common spoken English, most people would say "It is me" instead of "It is I." In contrast, transitive verbs take an object. For example, it would be correct to say "He pinched me," and it would be incorrect to say "He pinched I." In formal grammar, the verb **to be** serves as an exception to this rule for transitive verbs, but it is seldom followed (or known) in common spoken English. Most people would say "It is me" thinking that it is equivalent to "He pinched me," while in formal grammar these two cases are actually different.

**Directions:** Indicate if each boxed word is a direct object, object complement, indirect object, predicate adjective, or predicate nominative.

1) The rock broke the window .

2) He handed the kid a ball .

3) Hey! That pen is mine .

4) Her brother's eyes are blue .

5) She painted the flower pink .

6) You swept it under the rug.

7) The crowd soon became rowdy .

8) Exercise made the man tired .

9) The next day, Cindi called Heidi .

10) Find me tomorrow.

11) We named our hamster Hammy .

12) Tell her the news .

13) He opened the book to page 274.

14) Bring your friend Mason .

15) The barber cut his hair short .

16) The spectators were cheering .

17) Please hand me my phone .

18) Mom is paying the bills now.

19) The game sounded fun .

20) He ordered ceramic cookware .

21) Wash your sweaty, stinky socks .

22) Work will keep us busy.

23) The xerox machine is broken .

24) Give Wade a towel .

# PHRASES (challenge)

A **phrase** consists of two or more words that do **not** include both a subject and predicate (but it may include one of these). A phrase may act as a single part of speech or it may act as a single thought, but a phrase by itself is not a complete sentence.

- A **prepositional phrase** begins with a preposition and includes the object of the preposition (which is either a noun or a pronoun). Examples: to the store, for you, on the round table. A prepositional phrase can function as an adjective or an adverb. For example, in "Watch the child with the tricycle," the phrase **with the tricycle** functions as an adjective that describes the noun **child**, and in "We walked to the park," the phrase **to the park** functions as an adverb of place (it modifies the verb **walked**).

- An **adjective phrase** includes an adjective and words that modify, clarify, or enhance its meaning. Examples: ridiculously easy, so much brighter. An adjective phrase functions as an adjective. For example, in "The lecture was rather dull," the phrase **rather dull** functions as a predicate adjective (it describes the noun **lecture**) because **was** is a linking verb (it is a form of **to be**).

- An **adverb phrase** functions as an adverb. (An adverb phrase may also be another kind of phrase, such as a prepositional phrase.) Examples: at the park (adverb of place), before noon (adverb of time). Recall that an **adverb** modifies a verb, adjective, or another adverb. For example, in "He snorted like a pig," the phrase **like a pig** functions as an adverb of manner (it modifies the verb **snorted**), and in "Pick up your sister after school," the phrase **after school** functions as an adverb of time.

- A **noun phrase** includes a noun and words that modify, clarify, or enhance its meaning. Examples: the man's white t-shirt, the apartment above. A noun phrase functions as a noun. For example, in "My brown shoes are worn out," the phrase **My brown shoes** functions as a noun. Note: Compare the noun phrase **the apartment above** (which functions as a noun in "You could rent the apartment above") where **above** serves an adverb of place, with the prepositional phrase **above the apartment** (which functions as an adverb in "The drone hovered above the apartment") where **above** serves as a preposition.

- A **verb phrase** includes two or more verbs put together (including any auxiliary verbs or linking verbs). Examples: had said, are playing, could win, will have been reading. These verb phrases functions as verbs (contrast these with the participial and gerund phrases described below).

- A **participial phrase** includes a participle (which is a present or past tense form of a verb that functions as an adjective, meaning that it describes a noun or pronoun). Examples: dying of thirst, very tired, recently broken. Note: If the form of the verb ends with **ing**, it must function as an **adjective** to be part of a participial phrase (contrast this with the gerund phrase described below). For example, in "Trying his best, Seth sketched the person he had seen," **Trying** is a participle because it describes the noun **Seth**; the phrase **Trying his best** is a participial phrase.

- A **gerund phrase** includes a gerund (which is a form of a verb that ends with **ing** and which functions as a **noun**). Examples: playing after school, middleweight boxing. Note: A form of a verb ending with **ing** must function as an **noun** to be part of a gerund phrase (contrast this with the participial phrase described above). For example, in "Don't worry about crossing the bridge," **crossing** is a gerund because any preposition (such as **about**) takes a noun as an object; the phrase **crossing the bridge** is a gerund phrase.

- An **infinitive phrase** includes an infinitive (which includes the word **to** plus a verb). Recall that an infinitive may function as a noun, adjective, or adverb. Examples: to thank Dad, to go home.

- An **appositive phrase** includes an **appositive** (which is a noun or pronoun that refers to another noun or pronoun). For example, in "Shadow, a cat with black fur, loves to play with string," the noun **cat** is an appositive (it refers to the noun **Shadow**); the phrase **a cat with black fur** is an appositive phrase.

**Directions:** Write a sentence that uses the given phrase as directed.

1) Use "about astronomy" as an adjective.


2) Use "in the freezer" as an adverb.


3) Use "the dirty laundry" as a noun.


4) Use "would be feeling" as a verb.


5) Use "studying for the test" as an adjective.


6) Use "studying for the test" as a noun.


7) Use "to eat fruit" as a noun.


8) Use "a man on a mission" as an appositive.

# CLAUSES (challenge)

Unlike a phrase, a **clause** includes both a verb and its subject. A clause may act as a single part of speech or it may act as a portion of a sentence.

- An **independent clause** would form a complete sentence all by itself. For example, in the sentence "You may not leave until your chores are done," the clause **You may not leave** is an independent clause because it would form a complete sentence all by itself (whereas the phrase **until your chores are done** is a dependent clause).

- A **dependent clause** would **not** form a complete sentence all by itself. A dependent clause must be attached to another part of a sentence (such as an independent clause). A dependent clause is also called a **subordinate clause** because it generally begins with a **subordinating conjunction** (like because, unless, except, while, before, if, etc., or a phrase like "such as"). For example, in the sentence "You may not leave until your chores are done," the clause **until your chores are done** (which begins with the subordinating conjunction **until**) is a dependent clause because it has a subject and verb, but it would **not** form a complete sentence all by itself.

A **dependent clause** may function as a noun, adjective, or adverb.

- A **noun clause** may serve as the subject of the sentence, as the object of a (non-linking) verb, the object of a preposition, a predicate nominative (but **not** a predicate adjective), or as an appositive (recall the previous section). For example, in "I hope you find what you want," the dependent clause **what you want** (which begins with the subordinating conjunction **what**) is a noun clause because it is the direct object of the verb **find**.

- An **adjective clause** modifies a noun or pronoun. An adjective clause is also called a **relative clause** because it begins with a **relative pronoun** (which, who, whom, whose, that). For example, in "My camera, which I received as a gift, is in my backpack," the dependent clause **which I received as a gift** (which begins with the relative pronoun **which**) is an adjective clause because it describes the noun **camera**. Tip: In order to be a clause, it must include both a subject and a verb. Here, the subject is **I** and the verb is **received**.

- An **adverb clause** modifies a verb, adjective, or an adverb. It may indicate time, place, reason, purpose, condition, etc. For example, in "If you wash the dishes, I will cook dinner," the dependent clause **If you wash the dishes** (which begins with the subordinating conjunction **If**) provides a condition.

Clauses are either **restrictive** or **nonrestrictive**. (Some grammar guides use the terms **essential** and **nonessential** instead.)

- A clause is **restrictive** if it is essential for understanding the basic meaning of a sentence. If a restrictive clause is removed from the sentence, the basic meaning would be lost or altered. When a restrictive clause comes **after** a main clause, **no** comma is used. (However, when a dependent clause comes **before** a main clause, a comma separates the clauses whether it is restrictive or not.) For example, in "Any clothing that the chemicals may have touched must be discarded," the clause **that the chemicals may have touched** is restrictive. If this clause is removed, the basic meaning is different: "Any clothing must be discarded." Note: If a clause serves to **distinguish** one noun from others, it is considered to be restrictive. For example, in "The town where I grew up was featured in the movie," the clause **where I grew up** is restrictive because it identifies a particular town (which serves to distinguish it from other towns).

- A clause is **nonrestrictive** if it is **not** essential for understanding the basic meaning of a sentence. A nonrestrictive clause may be removed from the sentence without affecting its basic meaning. A comma is used to separate a nonrestrictive clause. For example, in "Canyon Lake, which I will visit on Sunday, lies on the other side of the hill," the clause **which I will visit on Sunday** is nonrestrictive because it provides additional information that is not necessary to the basic meaning. This clause may be removed: "Canyon Lake lies on the other side of the hill."

**Directions:** Circle the dependent clause in each sentence. Also, indicate whether the dependent clause functions as a noun, adjective, or adverb.

1) We won't be able to go on the trip unless we raise more money.

2) He exchanged the jacket because it was a size too small.

3) The person whose dog is loose should be more attentive.

4) While they waited in line, they discussed the upcoming election.

5) Don't add butter or cheese if you are trying to avoid dairy products.

6) You know what you did.

7) She wants to live where people are friendly.

8) What she wants can only be found in a specialty store.

9) When the repairman arrives, please send him upstairs to my office.

10) Three of the golf balls that you gave me are at the bottom of a pond.

11) Our neighbors raised their fence so that their dog couldn't escape.

12) The stadium, which the city plans to build, could seat 50,000 fans.

# TYPES OF SENTENCES (easy)

A **sentence** has a subject, has a predicate, and forms a complete thought. (Beware that the subject or predicate may be implied. For example, the subject is implied in the command "Come here.") A sentence can serve one of four different functions.

- A **declarative sentence** makes a statement (such as stating a fact) and ends with a period. Example: It is windy outside today.

- An **interrogative sentence** asks a question and ends with a question mark. Example: What is today's date?

- An **imperative sentence** makes a command, makes a request, gives direction, or gives advice or warning (without conveying strong emotion), and ordinarily ends with a period. The subject of an imperative sentence is often implied (as in the examples). Example: Please set the trash out. Second example: Watch for falling rocks.

- An **exclamatory sentence** conveys strong emotion and ends with an exclamation mark. Example: Wow! That is the best news ever!

**Directions:** For each sentence, indicate which kind it is.

1) When will you get paid?

2) I lost my favorite pencil.

3) We can't wait to get started!

4) See me before you leave.

5) Six times two equals twelve.

6) Why did you say that?

7) Keep your head steady.

8) Let go of my purse!

9) How have you been?

10) Try harder next time.

11) It had been an eventful week.

12) Look out for pedestrians.

13) I absolutely love it!

14) Is this your first bicycle?

# SENTENCE STRUCTURES (medium)

There are four types of sentence structures:

- A **simple sentence** consists of a single independent clause and no dependent clauses. Example: Melissa rode to school in a yellow bus.

- A **compound sentence** consists of two (or more) independent clauses and no dependent clauses. It either uses a **coordinating conjunction** (**and**, **or**, **but**, **nor**, **for**, **yet**, and **so**) or a semicolon (;). Example: He was late for work, yet he was reading the newspaper. Second example: The cat was happy to see her; it was feeding time.

- A **complex sentence** consists of a single independent clause and a single dependent clause (which uses a **subordinating conjunction**). Example: The dog won't leave you alone until you pet him.

- A **compound-complex sentence** consists of two (or more) independent clauses and at least one dependent clause. Example: If I visit, I won't be able to stay long; I have a long day tomorrow.

**Directions:** Indicate which structure each sentence has.

1) Every student in the class placed one bead on top of the front desk.

2) If you go on vacation this summer, bring back a little souvenir.

3) The woman wanted the laptop, but it seemed too expensive.

4) When it snows, the kids get excited; they love to build snowmen.

5) He bought a tie and a pair of shoes at the store.

6) Eileen sang, Tam danced, and Haley played the guitar.

7) We stopped at the gas station because one of the tires was low.

8) Do not disturb him unless there is an emergency; he needs his rest.

# FRAGMENT VS. RUN-ON (easy)

A <u>**sentence fragment**</u> is basically an incomplete sentence.

- A fragment may lack a <u>**subject**</u>. Example: Went to the store. The problem is that there is no subject. (Beware that an <u>**imperative sentence**</u> often has an implied subject. For example, "Go to the store" is a complete sentence with an implied subject.)

- A fragment may have an incomplete <u>**predicate**</u>. Example: The man a bottle to the child. The problem is that there is no <u>**verb**</u>. Second example: The woman brought. The problem is that the transitive verb <u>**brought**</u> requires an object (as in "The woman brought her son"). (Beware that some verbs may be used either in a transitive or intransitive sense. For example, in "I already ate," <u>**ate**</u> is intransitive, while in "I ate lunch," <u>**ate**</u> is transitive.)

- A fragment may be a <u>**dependent clause**</u> (beginning with a <u>**subordinating conjunction**</u>) disguised as a sentence. Example: Unless you hear otherwise. The word <u>**Unless**</u> functions as a subordinating conjunction. (Such a fragment is sometimes used when the writing is informal, but should only be done sparingly.)

- A fragment may form an <u>**incomplete thought**</u>. Example: The man drove to. The problem is that the preposition <u>**to**</u> needs an object.

A <u>**run-on sentence**</u> includes two (or more) independent clauses that do not correctly form a compound sentence.

- Some run-on sentences have independent clauses that run together without proper punctuation. Example: He rode his skateboard without protective gear he broke his arm. Following are three ways to correct this run-on sentence: insert a coordinating conjunction (a comma followed by **and**), insert a semicolon, or break it up into two shorter sentences.

- Some run-on sentences use a comma, but need a **conjunction** (either a coordinating conjunction like **and** or **but** or a subordinating conjunction like **because**). Example: Start packing now, our flight leaves in five hours. This could be improved by adding the subordinating conjunction **since** (in place of the comma).

- Some run-on sentences use the word **and** (or **but**) too many times. Example: I finished my homework and I walked the dog and I cleaned my room and I washed the car. This could be structured as a list using commas with a single **and**.

**Directions:** Is it a fragment, a run-on sentence, or a complete sentence?

1) Jackie left.

2) The girl with the long ponytail put.

3) We had a yard sale I sold my desk for $25.

4) Grabbed the man by his collar and whispered, "Please help me."

5) Although it would be nice to have the house painted.

6) Ed ate corn and Bo ate peas and Ty ate beets and Al ate carrots.

7) His toys spread throughout the house.

8) Since school ends early today, we have time to watch a movie.

9) The speckled horse across the stream through the forest.

10) Two young girls were in the backyard playing by.

11) Practice starts at 3:45 p.m. today the coach said not to be late.

12) Sing a song.

13) My parents gave me a yellow bike, I wanted a red one.

# SUBJECT-VERB AGREEMENT (medium)

Each **verb** must agree with its **subject** in both number and person. **Number** refers to whether the subject is **singular** or **plural**.

- Singular example: The girl works hard. The verb **works** agrees with the subject **girl**. There is just one girl. The verb **works** includes an **s**, but the noun **girl** doesn't.

- Plural example: The girls work hard. The verb **work** agrees with the subject **girls**. There are multiple girls. The verb **work** doesn't include an **s**, but the noun **girl** does.

**Person** refers to who the subject is.

- **First person** refers to the speaker; it is indicated by the pronoun **I** (singular) or **we** (plural).

- **Second person** refers to the person spoken to; it is indicated by the pronoun **you** (singular or plural). The pronoun **you** always takes the plural form of the verb, even if it refers to a single person. For example, one would say, "You are a great student," using the verb **are** (not the verb **is**) even though **you** is singular in this case.

- **Third person** refers to the person spoken about; it is indicated by the pronoun **he**, **she**, or **it** (singular), or the pronoun **they** (plural).

For a **regular** verb in the simple **present** tense, add an **s** only for the third person singular (contrast "I cook," "We cook," "You cook," and "They cook" with "He cooks," "She cooks," and "It cooks"). For a **regular** verb in the simple **past** tense, the verb ends with **ed** regardless of person ("I cooked," "We cooked," "You cooked", "He cooked," "She cooked," "It cooked," "They cooked"). Some verbs are **irregular**, meaning that they don't follow these rules; a few examples follow.

- Forms of **to be**: I am. We/You/They are. He/She/It is. I/He/She/It was. We/You/They were. (The slashes group sets together. For example, "We/You/They are" combines together "We are," "You are," and "They are.")

- Forms of **to have**: I/We/You/They have. He/She/It has. The simple past tense is always **had** (like "I had," "He had," and "They had").

- Forms of **to do**: I/We/You/They do. He/She/It does. The simple past tense is always **did**.

- For **modal helping verbs** (like **can** or **must**), **don't** add **s** to the third person singular verbs (compare "I can draw" with "He can draw").

A variety of situations can make subject-verb agreement seem somewhat tricky. Knowing the following rules and exceptions helps to get it right.

- Ignore any **phrases** that come between the subject and its verb. For example, in "That carton of eggs is sticky," the prepositional phrase **of eggs** may be ignored: "That carton is sticky." This makes it easy to see that the subject **carton** is singular. The verb **is** agrees with the singular subject **carton**. (Although **eggs** is plural, **eggs** is not the subject; the verb **is** goes with **carton**, not with **eggs**.)

- Treat a **compound subject** as a plural. If two (or more) subjects are joined by the word **and**, use the plural form of the verb. For example, in "His mother and father ride the bus each Monday," the compound subject **mother and father** acts as a plural noun (which requires using **ride** instead of **rides**). Exception: Rarely, a compound subject acts as a single unit. For example, in "Ham and cheese is today's sandwich special," **ham and cheese** is one kind of sandwich.

- If two singular subjects are joined by the word **or** (or the word **nor**), use the singular form of the verb. For example, in "Shelby or Violet has an appointment at eleven o'clock," each subject is singular (which requires using **has** instead of **have**). If two plural subjects are joined by the word **or** (or **nor**), use the plural form of the verb. For example, in "Tomatoes or mushrooms make a good soup base," the subject is plural (which requires using **make** instead of **makes**). If a singular subject and plural subject are joined by the word **or** (or **nor**), the subject nearest to the verb determines which form of the verb to use. For example, compare "Eggs or cereal is fine for breakfast" (where **is** goes with **cereal**) with "Cereal or eggs are fine for breakfast" (where **are** goes with **eggs**).

- Some indefinite **pronouns** (such as **few**, **several**, **both**, and **many**) are always **plural**. For example, in "Many of the campers are hungry," the indefinite pronoun **Many** is plural (which requires using **are** instead of **is**).

- Some indefinite **pronouns** (such as **each**, **everybody**, **nobody**, and **something**) are always **singular**. For example, in "Everything is ready now," the indefinite pronoun **everything** is singular (which requires using **is** instead of **are**).

- A small number of indefinite **pronouns** (including **all**, **any**, **more**, **most**, **none**, and **some**) are sometimes **singular** and sometimes **plural**. In this case, the verb must agree with the object of the preposition. (This is an exception to the prepositional phrase rule.) For example, compare "All of the pizza is gone" (where **is** goes with **pizza**) with "All of the cups are gone" (where **are** goes with **cups**).

- Many **collective nouns** (like **class**) are singular (as in "Class begins soon"), some (like **police**) are plural (as in "The police are investigating it"), and others (like **staff**) can be plural or singular depending on whether the members act as a single unit or separately (compare "The staff is marching with trays of food," where people act together, to "The staff are busy doing their own things until noon," where people act independently). **Tip**: When in doubt, refer directly to the individuals. For example, in "The members of the staff are busy doing their own things until noon," the subject is **members** (which is plural) and **staff** is part of a prepositional phrase.

- Beware that some nouns ending with **s** (like **politics**) are actually singular. For example, in "Politics is an interesting class," **politics** is a single subject.

- An **amount** (including time, money, measurements, etc.) is singular if it acts as one unit and plural otherwise. For example, in "Three days is a long time to wait," **three days** functions as a single period, while in "The last three days of school were rough," each of the **three days** was individually rough.

- When an **indefinite amount** is followed by the preposition **of** (including **half of**, **a lot of**, **a fraction of**, **a percentage of**, **some of**, and **most of**) and it is part of the subject, the verb must agree with the object of the preposition. (This is an exception to the prepositional phrase rule.) For example, compare "Half of the time has passed" (where **has** goes with **time**) with "Half of the students have left" (where **have** goes with **students**).

- When **each of** or **every one of** is part of the subject, it is singular (as in "Each of us has something to say"). When **the number of** is part of the subject, it is singular (as in "The number of days until my birthday is five"), but when **a number of** is part of the subject, it is plural (as in "A number of students are absent today").

- The main challenge with subject-verb agreement involves the **simple present tense** (compare "I eat" to "He eats"). The future tense is easy (compare "I will eat" to "He will eat"). The simple past tense of **to be** is irregular (compare "I was," "We were," and "He was"), but the simple past tense is easy for other verbs (compare "I ate" to "He ate"). For the progressive past tense or for a present tense that isn't simple, the main agreement issue is to use the correct form of the helping verbs **to be** or **to have** (compare "We have worked" to "He has worked" and "We were going" to "He was going").

**Directions:** For every slash, circle the correct form of each verb.

1) They was/were happy when it was/were clear and sunny.

2) I think/thinks that the tie with the stars go/goes best with that suit.

3) Please do/does not worry; he know/knows what I am/is/are doing.

4) They has/have gone fishing every time that he has/have come over.

5) My friends and I am/is/are skating today.

6) She say/says to please wait for her; she will/wills be here soon.

7) Either a waffle or a pancake is/are fine; both is/are delicious.

8) Nothing get/gets done when nobody want/wants to work.

9) One stack of papers is/are on your desk, and more is/are on the way.

10) Bacon, lettuce, and tomato is/are the sandwich of the day.

11) None of us was/were ready; all of the test was/were difficult.

12) I forget/forgets whether science or mathematics is/are her major.

13) He will give/gives us directions to the store when he call/calls.

14) Many of the guests is/are here. Most of the salsa is/are gone.

15) The team from the north has/have won every game this season.

16) Forty miles of desert sand lie/lies between the two cities.

17) The couple has/have two kids.

18) Half of the fruit was/were left. A third of the nuts was/were rotten.

# MOOD (challenge)

The **mood** of a verb shows the intention, attitude, or tone of the speaker (when written through the voice of a character or narrator) or the writer. There are three basic moods: indicative, imperative, and subjunctive.

The **indicative** mood states what appears to be (or what the speaker believes to be) a fact (including an opinion that is stated as if it were a fact). This is actually what most sentences do; the indicative is the most common mood. The examples below use the indicative.

- The baby **cried** when he **woke** up. (This is stated as a fact.)
- She **spoils** her baby. (This is an opinion, but it is stated as a fact.)

The **imperative** mood gives a command or makes a request. Generally, the command or request calls for action and is not just a light suggestion. The examples below use the imperative.

- **Bring** your phone here. (This commands you to action.)
- Do not **slam** the door. (This commands you to avoid an action.)
- After school, **come** straight home. (This commands you to action.)
- Please **wash** the dishes. (This request calls for action.)

The **subjunctive** mood either states what appears to be doubtful, highly unlikely, hypothetical, or contrary to fact, or it expresses a wish, demand, or request. In the subjunctive mood, the word **if** (or **unless**) is often present. A confusing feature of the subjunctive mood is that the verb usage often violates the usual rules for subject-verb agreement; for example, it uses **were** in place of **was** or uses **be** in place of **am**, **is**, or **are**.

- If I **were** you, I would ask my parents for help. (The first clause is contrary to fact and uses **were** instead of **was**.)

114

- Mr. Cooper requested that his assistant **be** available during the process. (This request is different from the imperative mood.)

Some texts also include additional moods, such as the conditional mood and the interrogative mood. The **conditional mood** includes a condition (often with a subordinate conjunction like **if**) and a helping verb (like **should**), as in "If you want to play golf today, we should leave soon." The **interrogative mood** asks a question while expressing uncertainty, as in "Will you be able to come to the banquet on Friday?"

**Directions:** Is the mood indicative, imperative, or subjunctive?

1) Raise your right hand up high.

2) I was standing nearby when it happened.

3) She threw the ball up in the air and it landed in the basket.

4) If I were in charge, I would make friendliness a priority.

5) They were here just a minute ago; I don't know where they went.

6) Please wash your hands before you touch anything.

7) If Dad were here, he would know what to do.

8) This baby is absolutely adorable.

9) I am going to the movie theater after I eat dinner.

10) Do not put paper or plastic material in the garbage can.

11) Ants were crawling all over the place.

12) If the tree were to fall, it would land on the roof of the house.

13) Please rescue our cat from the tree.

14) Kids were playing tag in the backyard.

15) The mayor requested that everyone be present for tonight's meeting.

# VOICE (challenge)

The **voice** of a transitive verb (which is a verb that takes an object) may be active or passive.

- In the **active voice**, the subject acts on the object. Example: A fox chased a rabbit.
- In the **passive voice**, the past participle of a verb is combined with a form of **to be** with the effect that the verb acts on the subject. Example: A rabbit was chased by a fox.

In general, the active voice is stronger, more direct, and easier for the reader to understand than the passive voice. Writing generally reads better in the active voice, though the passive voice can be effective when it is used appropriately and in moderation. An example of when it would be preferable to write "A rabbit was chased by a fox" instead of "A fox chased a rabbit" would be if writing from the rabbit's point of view.

**Directions:** Rewrite each sentence using the active voice.

1) He was patted on the back by his father.

2) The tree was struck by lightning.

3) Students were assigned seats.

4) My essay is being written.

5) Gina's purse was stolen by a homeless man.

6) The purse was found by the detective.

7) Every day, many coins are thrown into the pond.

8) Your suggestion will be given consideration.

# PRONOUN MISTAKES (medium)

Recall that a **pronoun** is a word that refers to a noun that was already used in the same sentence or a previous sentence. The **antecedent** is the word that the pronoun refers to. For example, in "That eraser is mine," the pronoun **mine** refers to the antecedent **eraser**. Following are a variety of ways that pronouns should or shouldn't be used. It may help to review the section entitled "Pronouns."

- A pronoun should be used to **reduce** the **repetition** of a noun. For example, "My bike had a flat tire, so my dad fixed it" sounds better than "My bike had a flat tire, so my dad fixed my bike." In the first case, the pronoun **it** helps to avoid repeating the noun **bike**.

- Be careful not to include both the pronoun and its antecedent unnecessarily. For example, in "My friend she is a good gymnast," the pronoun **she** should be removed.

- Avoid **vague pronoun references**; ensure that the antecedent will be clear to the reader. For example, in "Gloria and Anita went to the store because she was out of cookies," the pronoun **she** is vague; it isn't clear whether Gloria or Anita is out of cookies. Contrast this with "Because Gloria was out of cookies, she went to the store with Anita," where the pronoun **she** clearly refers to Gloria. As another example, in "They clean the street on Monday mornings," the pronoun **They** is vague (unless the antecedent was made clear in a previous sentence).

- Check that the pronoun refers to the **correct antecedent**. For example, in "After discussing the problem with his partners, Mr. Allen decided to sue them," the pronoun **them** seems to refer to his partners. The correct meaning is clear when the sentence is worded

- The personal pronouns **I**, **we**, **you**, **he**, **she**, **it**, and **they** are used as **subjects**, while the personal pronouns **me**, **us**, **you**, **him**, **her**, **it**, and **them** are used as **objects** (of transitive verbs or prepositions). For example, in "She gave it to us," **She** is the subject, **it** is the object of the verb **gave**, and **us** is the object of the preposition **to**. It would be incorrect to begin this sentence "Her gave" (since **She** is a subject, whereas **Her** is an object) or to finish this sentence "to we" (since **we** is a subject, whereas **us** is an object). This rule also applies to compound subjects or objects. For example, compare "Lori and I ate spaghetti" (where **Lori and I** are subjects) to "The sound startled Lori and me" (where **Lori and me** are objects).

- The pronouns **who** and **whoever** are used as **subjects**, while the pronouns **whom** and **whomever** are used as **objects** (of transitive verbs or prepositions). For example, compare "Who made this mess?" (where **who** is a subject, since you might answer the question "He made this mess," but wouldn't say "Him made this mess") to "To whom should I address the letter?" (where **whom** is the object of the preposition; you might answer the question "To him," but wouldn't answer the question "To he").

- The **number** of a pronoun (or possessive adjective) must agree with its antecedent; they must either both be **plural** or both be **singular**. For example, in "I finished my homework, but left it at home," the pronoun **it** and the antecedent **homework** are both singular, whereas in "The players discussed why they lost the game," the pronoun **they** and the antecedent **players** are both plural.

- The **gender** of a pronoun (or possessive adjective) must agree with its antecedent (when the gender of the antecedent is clearly known). For example, in "Ms. Singh hired a mechanic to fix her car," the possessive adjective **her** and the antecedent **Ms. Singh** are both feminine.

- The pronoun used in a comparison following the words **than** or **as** can significantly alter the meaning of a sentence. For example, compare "Dad likes baseball more than me" (which means that the father likes the sport more than he likes his child) with "Dad likes baseball more than I do" (which means that the father likes the sport more than his child likes the sport).

- **Possessive pronouns** (like **mine** and **theirs**) and **possessive adjectives** (like **my, their,** or **whose**) indicate a sense of belonging. For example, in "Monika lost her umbrella," the possessive adjective **her** indicates that the umbrella is Monika's.

**Directions:** For every slash, circle the correct pronoun or adjective.

1) We/Us gave Sylvia a bracelet on her/hers birthday.

2) Jason and I/me went to the show. They gave we/us free goggles.

3) Dad brought me/my friends and I/me to the park.

4) She/Her lost her/hers ring last month. She/Her found it/them today.

5) Mr. Ferguson shook his/her head in disbelief.

6) Who/Whom called when I/me was in the bathroom?

7) With who/whom did you/your dance?

8) Adam's grandmother left his/her dentures on the counter.

9) I/Me found grapes in the refrigerator; I/me ate all of it/them.

10) That/those seat is my/mine. Please find your/yours own.

11) Whoever/Whomever figured that out is a genius.

# MODIFIER MISTAKES (medium)

<u>Modifiers</u> are words, phrases, or clauses that function as **adjectives** (which modify nouns) or **adverbs** (which modify verbs, adjectives, or other adverbs). Following are a few mistakes that are commonly made with modifiers. It may help to review the sections on phrases and clauses.

- When a modifier is in the wrong place, it may appear to modify the wrong word. This is called a **misplaced modifier**. For example, compare "Murphy crashed into a trash can that was nearly full" with "Murphy nearly crashed into a trash can that was full," where **nearly** modifies different words ("nearly crashed" versus "nearly full"). As another example, compare "Janice wondered why bears hibernate during class" with "During class, Janice wondered why bears hibernate," where **during class** modifies different parts of the sentence (whether "Janice is wondering during class" or if "bears are hibernating during class").

- A special kind of misplaced modifier occurs when the word being modified is absent. This is called a **dangling modifier**. For example, in "Soaking wet from the rain, the fireplace was turned on," the person who is soaking wet is not mentioned in the sentence. Compare this to "Soaking wet from the rain, Malcolm turned the fireplace on."

- When a modifier can modify words on either side of it, this can create confusion. This is called a **two-way modifier** (or a **squinting modifier**). For example, in "Dancing frequently makes my hips sore," it is not clear whether the meaning is "Frequent dancing causes sore hips" or if the meaning is "Dancing causes sore hips most of the time."

120

**Directions:** In each sentence, the boxed modifier either creates possible confusion or does not produce the intended meaning. Rewrite each sentence to avoid confusion or to produce a clear (or different) meaning.

1) The kid was tall enough to almost ride the roller coaster.

2) Jared's boss told him in the morning he could visit the doctor.

3) Starving after chopping firewood, pizza was ordered.

4) A man was riding a bicycle with a mustache.

5) Dawn asked her brother why he climbed the tree while eating dinner.

6) A boy was riding a skateboard in jeans and a t-shirt.

7) Lydia remembered to barely turn in her homework assignment.

8) Singing in the shower, it was hard for everyone else to concentrate.

9) Her boss said before work she would be evaluated.

# COMMON WORD MIX-UPS (medium)

Following are some words that are often confused, along with tips for choosing the right word.

- **it's/its**: Use **it's** if it would make sense to replace it with **it is**, as in "It's snowing" (which could be written "It is snowing"). Use **its** to mean "belonging to it," as in "The bird is sitting in its nest" (where "it is nest" wouldn't make sense).

- **you're/your**: Use **you're** if it would make sense to replace it with **you are**, as in "You're late" (which could be written "You are late"). Use **your** to mean "belonging to you," as in "May I borrow your pencil?" (where "you are pencil" wouldn't make sense).

- **they're/their/there**: Use **they're** if it would make sense to replace it with **they are**, as in "They're in the garage" (which could be written "They are in the garage"). Use **their** to mean "belonging to them," as in "Their uniforms are dirty" (where "They are uniforms" wouldn't make sense). Use **there** to refer to a place (or time or matter), as in "Place the book over there."

- **to/too/two**: Use **to** as a preposition with a noun or pronoun as an object, as in "Drive to the store." Use **too** for something additional, as in "Bring one for me, too," or for emphasis, as in "It is too early for that." Use **two** for the number 2, as in "Our house has two bathrooms."

- **lay/lie**: Use **lay** to mean "to put" or "to place" as a transitive verb with a noun or pronoun as an object, as in "Lay the book on the desk." The simple past tense of **lay** is **laid**, as in "He laid the book on the desk earlier," and the past participle is also **laid**, as in "He has already laid the book on the desk." Use **lie** to mean "to rest" as an intransitive verb (which has no object), as in "Lie down for a while." The simple past tense of **lie** is **lay**, as in "He lay down a while ago," and the past participle is **lain**, as in "Every day this week, he has lain down for a while after coming home from work." (For the other meaning of **lie**, "to not tell the truth," the simple past tense and past participle are both **lied**.)

- **who's/whose**: Use **who's** if it would make sense to replace it with **who is**, as in "Who's at the door?" (which could be written "Who is at the door?"). Use **whose** to mean "belonging to whom," as in "Whose key is this?" (where "Who is key" wouldn't make sense).

- **who/whom**: Use **who** as a subject (which performs the action of the verb), as in "Who used my eraser?" Use **whom** as an object (of a transitive verb or a preposition), as in "For whom did you bake the bread?" (where **whom** is the object of the preposition **for**). **Tip**: A question with **who** can be answered with **he** (or **she**), while a question with **whom** can be answered with **him** (or **her**). For example, "He used my eraser" answers "Who used my eraser?" and "You baked the bread for him" answers "For whom did you bake the bread."

- **good/well**: Use **good** as an adjective to describe a noun or pronoun, as in "She is a good person" (where **good** describes the noun **person**) or "Broccoli is good for you" (where **good** is a predicate adjective). Use **well** as an adverb to modify a verb, adjective, or other adverb, as in "Your son did well in my class" (where **well** modifies the verb **did**). Exception: When **well** means better health or wellness, **well** is an adjective. For example, after surgery a person might say, "I am **well**," where **well** is a predicate adjective.

- **less/fewer**: Use **less** with singular words, as in "He has less milk than me." Use **fewer** with plural words, as in "He has fewer pancakes than me."

- **between/among**: Use **between** when dividing into two parts, as in "The land was divided between his two sons." Use **among** when dividing into more than two parts, as in "The land was divided among his three daughters."

- **passed/past**: Use **passed** as a verb, as in "Time passed by faster than he expected." Use **past** as another part of speech, as in "In the past, the city was not nearly as populated as it is now" (where **past** is a noun) or "This past week was full of surprises" (where **past** is an adjective that describes the noun **week**).

- **except/accept**: Use **except** to exclude something, as in "Everyone was present except for me." Use **accept** for other meanings, as in "Please accept my apology."

- **affect/effect**: Use **affect** (almost always) as a verb to indicate a change, as in "Don't let his comments affect your mood." Use **effect** (usually) as a noun to indicate a result, as in "The soft paint color seemed to have a calming effect on people."

- **principle/principal**: Use **principle** for an idea such as a belief or law, as in "According to Fermat's principle, light takes the path of least time." Use **principal** to mean major (including the person who runs a school), as in "My principal reason for becoming a doctor was to help people."

**Directions:** For each word choice, circle the correct word.

1) According to your/you're watch, its/it's currently a quarter passed/past four.

2) Whose/Who's tapping the desk? Its/It's really affecting/effecting my concentration.

3) The principal/principle presented awards to/too/two students who performed very good/well in their/there/they're courses.

4) There/Their/They're was no good/well reason for there to be fewer/less nurses working at the hospital this year.

5) She was accepted/excepted into to/too/two different summer programs that introduce the principals/principles of coding.

6) There/Their/They're sad stories about the hardships they faced while growing up really affected/effected me, to/too/two.

7) You must choose among/between Cameron and Brady; there/their/they're the only to/too/two players remaining.

8) With who/whom did you go to/too/two the dance? It seems like everyone went accept/except for me.

9) They already accepted/excepted there/their/they're invitations to the birthday party. Its/It's to/too/two late to change the date.

10) One side affect/effect of the medicine was that she had fewer/less energy than usual.

11) Who/Whom passed/past you just before the race ended? I would like to watch the to/too/two of you race again.

12) "Your/You're responsible for dividing the chores among/between yourselves," the father said to/too/two his three children.

13) Whose/Who's turn is it to lay/lie down on the hammock? My brother would like a turn, to/too/two.

14) Lay/lie the rug in the middle of the living room for now. We can adjust its/it's position later.

15) The patient laid/lay/lied down for a nap half an hour ago. He was not feeling good/well after he received his shot.

16) She laid/lay/lied her notebook on the table and opened the refrigerator. Unfortunately, there/their/they're was nothing good/well to eat.

# ANSWER KEY

## Common Nouns

1) children, fun, kite, beach, day

2) earrings, blouse

3) rule, park, dog, leash

4) Students, place, library

5) doctor, cup, morning, weeks

6) curiosity, cows, corral

7) items, game, glove, shoes, hat

8) invitation, date, time, location

9) Yesterday, food, cafeteria

10) hiker, path, woods, bridge

11) evening, girl, time, show

12) hours, rain, sun, ascent

13) beginning, movie, action

Note: Compare the use of the word **beginning** in Exercises 12 and 13.

In Exercise 12, it is a verb, but in Exercise 13, it is a noun.

14) thought, sailor, option

## Proper Nouns

1) Ms. Jimenez, Revolutionary War

2) Austin, Texas

3) I, Harbor Middle School

4) Dr. Williams

5) Blueridge Farms

6) November, St. Francis Hospital

7) Second Avenue, Phoenix, Arizona

8) Crest, Amazon, Sunday, Monday

9) Lisa, Anna, Grand Canyon

10) Pike's Peak, Colorado

11) *Snow White*, Halloween

12) Thursday, Dad, Nike, Mall of America

13) I, Mom, Keith

Note: **Dad** is a proper noun in Exercise 12 where it is used as the name of the father (and similarly **Mom** is a proper noun in Exercise 13), whereas **dad** is a common noun in Exercise 13. The expression **your dad** in Exercise 13 does not use **dad** as a name.

## Plurals

| | | |
|---|---|---|
| 1) televisions | 2) valleys | 3) deer |
| 4) branches | 5) tomatoes | 6) leaves |
| 7) ratios | 8) babies | 9) sprinklers |
| 10) women | 11) lives | 12) trios |
| 13) salmon | 14) addresses | 15) ponies |
| 16) hooves/hoofs | 17) geese | 18) radii/radiuses |
| 19) essays | 20) taxes | 21) mice |
| 22) bonuses | 23) avocados/avocadoes | 24) halves |
| 25) chapters | 26) media | 27) leashes |
| 28) alumni | 29) beliefs | 30) vertebrae |

Note: **beliefs** is a plural noun, whereas **believes** is a verb.

| | | |
|---|---|---|
| 31) oxen | 32) viruses | 33) indices/indexes |

## Collective Nouns

1) team (a group of players), set (a group of drills)

2) litter (a group of puppies), pile (a group of leaves)

3) crew (a group of sailors), fleet (a group of ships)

4) flock (a group of birds), forest (a group of trees)

5) flight (a group of stairs)

6) family (a group of relatives), swarm (a group of bees)

7) Management (a group of supervisors), union (a group of employees)

8) chain (a series of objects), archipelago (a group of islands)

9) class (a group of students), duets (pairs of musicians), quartets (groups of four musicians)

10) collection (a group of objects), library (a group of books)

Note: In this sentence, **library** refers to a group of books (not to a building where people go to borrow books).

11) bale (a pile of hay), livestock (a group of certain kinds of animals)

12) alliance (a group of entities working toward a common objective)

13) array (an orderly arrangement), galaxy (a group of stars)

14) panel (a group of people serving a specific purpose), government (a group of people or agencies that control the affairs of a region), weekend (a pair of days: Saturday and Sunday)

## Pronouns

1) that (relative), I (personal), his (possessive)

The relative pronoun **that** often serves a function similar to a conjunction. When **that** is the object or subject of a verb, it functions (at least partly) as a pronoun. Here, **that** is the object of the verb **found**.

2) Those (demonstrative), that (relative; see the answer to Exercise 1), anyone (indefinite)

3) She (personal), mine (possessive), yours (possessive)

4) What (interrogative), me (personal), nothing (indefinite)

5) you (personal), it (personal), We (personal), this (demonstrative), ourselves (reflexive)

6) They (personal), Theirs (possessive)

7) That (demonstrative), I (personal), anyone (indefinite),

who (relative; see the answer to Exercise 1), it (personal)

8) us (personal), anything (indefinite), we (personal), you (personal)

9) Those (demonstrative), that (relative; see the answer to Exercise 1), I (personal)

10) You (personal), yourselves (reflexive), Few (indefinite)

11) ours (possessive), Whose (interrogative), it (personal)

12) them (personal), others (indefinite)

Note: In this case, **few** is an adjective (not a pronoun) because it modifies the noun **solutions**.

13) whom (relative; see the answer to Exercise 1), she (personal)

Note: In this case, **this** is an adjective (not a pronoun) because it modifies the noun **cake**.

14)  That (demonstrative), one (indefinite), I (personal)

In this case, **which** is an adjective (not a pronoun) because it modifies the noun **orange**.

## Possessive

1) dog's leash, dad's truck (both singular)

2) boys' moms (**boys** is plural, **school bus** does not use an apostrophe)

3) women's locker room (an irregular plural)

4) boss's wife's purse (the purse that belongs to the wife of the boss)

5) brother's room (**hers** does not have an apostrophe)

6) forest's trees (collective noun treated as singular)

7) students' golf bags (plural), school's name (singular)

8) aunt and uncle's only car (the aunt and uncle have joint possession)

9) pitcher's and shortstop's autographs (two separate autographs)

10) boys' and girls' (both plural and their bathrooms are separate)

11) Jeffersons' cats (plural), Mr. King's (singular)

12) Zach and Kayla's twin daughters (Zach and Kayla are the parents)

13) Ms. Bailey's and Ms. Hope's pools (two separate pools)

14) people's court (**cousins** and **defendants** are just plural nouns)

## Abstract Nouns

1) colors (concrete; you can see them), painting (concrete; you can view it; used here to refer to a specific piece of artwork, not a process or subject), joy (abstract; an emotion)

2) penalty (abstract; an idea), referee (concrete; you can see him), whistle (concrete; you can hear it)

3) fragrance (concrete; you can smell it), delight (abstract; an emotion), nose (concrete; you can see it)

4) breeze (concrete; you can feel it), evenings (abstract; a time period), summer (abstract; a time period)

5) disgust (abstract; an emotion), taste (concrete; you can sense it with your tongue), fruit (concrete; you can taste it)

6) woman (concrete; you can see her), courage (abstract; a quality)

7) telescope (concrete; you can see it), nebula (concrete; you can see it through a telescope), crab (concrete; you can see it)

8) style (abstract; a quality; used here in a general sense), industry (abstract; a quality), creativity (abstract; a quality)

9) government (abstract; used here in a general sense), religion (abstract; a belief), history (abstract; a school subject)

10) love (abstract; an emotion), design (concrete; you can see it; used here to refer to specific artwork that can be seen, not used in a general sense), jacket (concrete; you can wear it)

11) vacation (abstract; an idea), surprise (abstract; a quality)

12) wisdom (abstract; a quality), war (abstract; an idea), peace (abstract; a quality)

13) jury (concrete; you can see them; used here to refer to specific

people), defendant (concrete; you can meet this person); law (abstract; an idea)

## Action Verbs

1) Believe (mental), swims (physical), won (physical; he swam fastest)

2) paint (physical), Choose (mental)

3) wished (mental), play (physical) Note: **to** + verb (like "to play") forms an infinitive. We will discuss infinitives after learning more about verbs.

4) told (physical; he spoke), worry (mental)

5) hopes (mental), dances (physical)

6) memorized (mental), forgot (mental)

7) stared (physical; keeping eyes open is physical), blinking (physical)

8) planned (mental), meet (physical; getting together in person is physical), rang (physical)

9) said (physical; she spoke), remember (mental), set (physical)

10) escaping (physical; it involved moving), needed (mental), hide (physical; it involves moving into a certain position and then not moving)

11) decided (mental), enjoy (mental)

12) Stop (physical; the act of stopping a physical activity), weeping (physical; tears are falling), breathe (physical; lungs are working), think (mental)

13) Surprised (mental), expected (mental), confuse (mental)

14) sympathized (mental), yelled (physical), Stop (mental; the act of stopping a mental activity, unlike Exercise 12), judging (mental)

15) wants (mental), speak (physical), regarding (mental)

## Transitive Verbs

1) spilled (transitive; milk is the object that spilled)

2) received (transitive; driver's license is what she received), drives (intransitive; she drives, but **she** is the subject, not the object)

3) sit (intransitive), read (transitive; chapters are what were read)

4) called (transitive; Mr. Gomez was called), spoke (intransitive)

5) set (transitive; the map was set), pacing (intransitive)

6) walk (intransitive), Run (intransitive), begins (intransitive; the movie is what begins, and **movie** is the subject, not the object)

7) chose (transitive; Pria was chosen), agreed (intransitive)

8) taught (transitive; secret handshake was taught)

Note: Here, **meeting** functions as a noun, not a verb.

9) give (intransitive; the two words **give up** are a phrasal verb, meaning that together they act similar to the single word **surrender**; there is not a noun here acting as an object of **give**; the team is what might give up), injured (transitive; foot was injured)

10) threw (transitive; magazines were thrown)

11) sent (transitive; book is what was sent; book is the direct object, while Stephen is the indirect object; Stephen was not sent, the book was; this sentence can be rewritten as, "Elizabeth sent his mother's favorite recipe book to Stephen")

**Tip: To find the direct object of a transitive verb, ask the question, "The subject (verb) what?"** For Exercise 11, the subject is Elizabeth and the verb is **sent**. The question is, "Elizabeth sent what?" The answer is that a book was sent.

12) remember (transitive; time was remembered; although remember is often intransitive, as in, "Yes, I remember," it can also be transitive, as in, "I remember it"), caught (transitive, catfish were caught)

13) brought (transitive; the dog was brought; imagine rewriting the first part of the sentence as, "Maddie brought the dog home"; the dog is what was brought, whereas home is where the dog was brought; the object of a transitive verb answers who or what), ate (transitive; food was eaten)

## To Be

1) were, was     2) had been (note that **had eaten** is not a form of **to be**)

3) am, Were     4) being, is     5) could be, is

6) are (since **we're** is a contraction of **we are**)

7) am (since **I'm** is a contraction of **I am**), will be

8) be     9) is, are     10) wouldn't be

11) are (since **you're** is a contraction of **you are**), have been

12) am, is, are, be     13) would be, are

14) must have been, had been

## Linking Verbs

1) sounded (linking; "The nurse was sincere" makes sense)

2) seems (linking; "That movie is scary" makes sense)

3) tasted (action; "I never was Meg's lasagna" does not make sense)

4) felt (linking; "He was sleepy after work" makes sense)

5) were (linking; **were** is a form of **to be**)

6) turned (action; "We were right at the signal" does not make sense)

7) remain (linking; "Please be calm" makes sense)

8) smell (linking; "These peaches are fresh" makes sense)

9) became (linking; "Mark Twain is/was famous" makes sense)

10) grew (action; "Mr. Jay was a mustache" does not make sense)

11) proven (action; "We were him wrong" does not make sense)

12) looks (linking; "Her leg is fine now" makes sense)

## Helping Verbs

1) were (tense)     2) did (mood; indicative)

3) had been (tense)     4) was (voice; **given** is a past participle)

5) will be (tense)     6) may (possibility/permission)

7) could (possibility)     8) will be (voice; **seen** is a past participle)

9) have been (tense)

10) must (necessity)

11) will (tense)

12) Did (mood; interrogative; part of Didn't)

## Verbals

1) checkered (past participle; adjective; describes the pants), soaking (present participle; part of the compound verb **are soaking**); washing (present participle; adjective; describes the machine)

2) Boating (gerund; noun; the subject of **turned out**); charming (present participle; adjective; describes the man); claimed (past participle; part of the compound verb **had claimed**)

Note: turned is a simple past tense verb (it is **not** a participle, even though the past participle form of this verb is spelled the same as the simple past tense form). If the sentence said "had turned" rather than simply "turned," then **turned** would be a past participle (part of the compound verb **had turned**).

3) vacationing (gerund; noun; the object of the verb **enjoyed**); camping (present participle; adjective; describes the supplies)

Note: enjoyed is a simple past tense verb (see the note to Exercise 2).

4) waving (present participle; adjective; describes the man), rowing (present participle; adjective; describes the team)

5) Screaming (present participle; adjective; describes the kids), frozen (past participle; adjective; describes the lemonade)

6) shouting (gerund; noun; the subject of the verb **woke**), terrifying (present participle; adjective; describes the nightmare)

7) Surprised (past participle; adjective; describes the man), padded (past participle; adjective; describes the chair)

8) leaning (present participle; adjective; describes the tree); planted (past participle; part of the compound verb **was planted**)

9) sealed (past participle; adjective; describes the envelope), sitting (present participle; adjective; describes the person)

10) singing (gerund; noun), unexpected (past participle; adjective; describes the **noun** delight)

11) said (past participle; part of the compound verb **had said**), frosted (past participle; adjective; describes the glasses), dining (present participle; adjective; describes the table)

12) hiking (gerund; noun), ziplining (gerund; noun); rafting (gerund; noun), roaring (present participle; adjective; describes the rapids, which refers to a portion of a river with swift current)

13) Shouted (past participle; adjective; describes the words), meant (past participle; part of the compound verb **are meant**), smiling (present participle; adjective; describes the faces)

## Infinitives

1) to play (noun; the object of **want**)
Note: This sentence structure is subject + verb + infinitive.

2) to purchase (adjective; describes the supplies)
Note: This sentence structure is subject + verb + object + infinitive.

3) to fish (adjective; describes the places)
Note: This sentence structure is subject + verb + object + infinitive.

4) To listen (noun; the subject of the compound verb **is considered**)
Note: This sentence structure is infinitive + comp. verb + adjective.

5) to remain (adverb; modifies the verb **eat**; explains why you should eat vegetables; the infinitive phrase **to remain healthy** functions as an adverb)
Note: This sentence structure is verb + noun + infinitive phrase.

6) To relax (adverb; modifies the verb **listens**; explains why she listens)
Note: This sentence structure is inf. + comma + subj. + verb + obj.
Note: The last **to** is not part of an infinitive; music is not a verb.

7) to do (adjective; describes the work, which is a noun in this sentence)

Note: This sentence structure is subject + verb + object + infinitive.

8) to dance (adverb; modifies the verb **came**; explains why he came there)

Note: This sentence structure is subject + verb + object + infinitive.

9) to buy (adverb; modifies the verb **went**; explains why I went to the store; the infinitive phrase **to buy food** functions as an adverb)

Note: This sentence structure is subject + verb + object + inf. phrase.

Note: The first **to** is not part of an infinitive; the store is not a verb.

10) to skate (noun; the object of the verb **loves**)

11) **to** must be omitted (everyone watched the teams play)

When an infinitive follows the verb **watch**, **to** is omitted.

12) **to** is optional (please help me to clean or please help me clean)

When an infinitive follows the verb **help**, **to** is optional.

13) **to** must be omitted (I can fix any problem)

When an infinitive follows the modal helping verb **can**, **to** is omitted.

14) **to** must be omitted (You must wash your hands)

When an infinitive follows the modal helping verb **must**, **to** is omitted.

15) **to** is required (We need to hear both sides)

Unlike the verb **must**, the verb **need** requires the word **to**. It is instructive to compare Exercises 14–15. The verb **need** is a semi-modal verb because it does not quite behave the same way as the verb **must**.

16) **to** must be omitted (Did you hear my daughter sing)

When an infinitive follows the verb **sing**, **to** is omitted.

## Principal Parts

1) baked (past tense), bring (present infinitive)

2) swing (present infinitive), keep (present infinitive)

Note: Don't let the word **infinitive** confuse you. Any verb used in the simple present tense uses the **present infinitive** part of the verb, even when the verb is not used as an infinitive. It gets this name because the verb has the same form (apart from a possible **s** at the end) when used in the simple present tense or as an infinitive. That is, if the sentence had said, "To swing a golf club," **swing** would be spelled the same as it is in, "When you swing the golf club."

3) looking (present participle), find (present infinitive), watched (past participle; the word **had** shows this is past participle, not past tense)

Note: The **ing** form of the verb is called the **present participle** even if it is used in the past tense like **was looking**.

Note: In a compound verb, the words **has**, **had**, and **have** help to distinguish the **past participle** from the **past tense** form of the verb. (The words **has**, **had**, and **have** can also be used with the **present participle**, but there the **ing** distinguishes it from the **past participle**.)

4) announced (past tense), fits (present infinitive)

Note: The simple present tense sometimes adds an **s** to the present infinitive form of the verb. The infinitive is **to fit**. Compare this with I fit, you fit, he fits, she fits, it fits, we fit, and they fit.

5) waiting (present participle), buy (present infinitive)

6) left (past participle; part of the compound verb **had left**; the word **had** shows this is past participle, not past tense), arrived (past tense)

7) remembers (present infinitive), happened (past tense), came (past tense)

8) risen (past participle), returns (present infinitive)

9) telling (present participle), lost (past tense), said (past tense), listen (present infinitive; part of the compound verb **will not listen**)

10) Wake (present infinitive), arriving (present participle)

Note: Here, **past** functions as an adjective (not as a verb).

11) found (past participle; part of the compound verb **has found**; the word **has** shows this is past participle, not past tense)

12) slide (present infinitive), rounds (present infinitive)

13) flying (present infinitive), sold (past participle; the word **have** shows this is past participle, not past tense)

## Verb Tense

1) ends (simple present), will meet (simple future)

2) had thrown (past perfect), learned (simple past), were (simple past)

3) will have been attending (future perfect progressive)

4) were building (past progressive), are testing (present progressive)

5) have scored (present perfect)

6) Believe (simple present), will be visiting (future progressive)

7) have been searching (present perfect progressive), woke (simple past)

8) Eat (simple present), will have begun (future perfect), arrives (simple present)

9) had been reading (past perfect progressive), wrote (simple past)

10) am waiting (present progressive; **am** is part of **I'm**), will call (simple future), buy (simple present)

11) had heard (past perfect), reached (simple past)

12) retires (simple present), will have been working (future perfect progressive)

13) has found (perfect present)

## Irregular Verbs

1) was/were, been

2) began, begun

3) broke, broken

4) caught, caught

5) came, come

6) did, done

Compare: He **came** to dinner. She **had come** earlier.

7) drew, drawn

8) drank, drunk

9) drove, driven

10) ate, eaten

11) felt, felt

12) found, found

13) flew, flown

14) froze, frozen

15) got, gotten (or got)

16) gave, given

Note: Dictionaries include **got** as an alternative to **gotten** for the past participle of **get**.

17) went, gone

18) heard, heard

19) hid, hidden (or hid)

20) kept, kept

21) knew, known

22) laid, laid (but **not** lain)

23) left, left

24) lay, lain (compare with 22)

Notes: The verbs **to lay** (meaning to put) and **to lie** (meaning to rest) are easy to confuse unless you remember that **to lay** is transitive (it takes an object) and **to lie** is intransitive (it doesn't take an object). The forms of **to lay** are **lay**, **laid**, and **laid**; the past tense and past participle are the same. Examples: I now **lay** my book on the table. Yesterday, I **laid** my book on the table. Previously, I **have laid** my book on the table. The forms of **to lie** are **lie**, **lay**, and **lain**. (One thing that is confusing is that the past tense of **lie** is **lay**.) Examples: I now **lie** on a blanket. Yesterday, I **lay** on a blanket. Previously, I **have lain** on a blanket.

25) paid, paid

26) rode, ridden

27) rang, rung

28) rose, risen

29) said, said

30) saw, seen

31) sought, sought

32) sold, sold

33) shook, shaken

34) shrank*, shrunk*

Note: **Shrank** or **shrunk** are acceptable past tense forms of **shrink**, while **shrunk** or **shrunken** are acceptable past participles.

35) spoke, spoken

36) stood, stood

37) stole, stolen

38) swore, sworn

39) took, taken

40) thought, thought

41) threw, thrown

42) wore, worn

## Adjectives

1) Numerous, colorful, cork (meaning that the board is made of cork)

2) long, brown, fastest (superlative), our (possessive)

Note: Two (or more) adjectives can modify the same noun.

3) checkered, denim, jogging

4) These (demonstrative), hard, frustrated

5) dozen, nonfat, fresh, ten (quantitative)

6) Your (possessive), friendlier (comparative), My (possessive), his, sharp

7) beige, soft (**looks** is a linking verb), fluffy, expensive

8) Whose (interrogative), This (demonstrative), that (demonstrative), clean (**was** is a linking verb; **clean** modifies the noun **desk**)

9) bored, interesting (postpositive), fun (**sounds** is a linking verb)

10) Every (distributive), his (possessive), messy, last (modifies **year**)

11) One (quantitative), spiral, Another (modifies **time**), glass

Note: Some words can function as nouns or adjectives depending on how they are used. For example, compare "I have **one** key" with "**One** of us is lying," and compare "It is a **glass** pane" with "He broke the **glass**."

12) Our (possessive), German (proper), first (modifies **place**), her (possessive), good (modifies **behavior**)

13) many (quantitative), southern, those (demonstrative)

14) calm, quiet, any (distributive), sudden

15) Your (possessive), high-pitched (compound), pleasant

16) excited, original, all (modifies **week**)

Note: Here, **most** functions as an adverb (since it modifies the adjective **original**), not as an adjective (since it doesn't modify the noun **idea**).

17) That (demonstrative), shiny, broken, fine

Note: **these** functions as a pronoun in this sentence; it is not used as an adjective here because it does not modify a noun. Compare "**These** are fine" with "**These** earrings are fine."

18) our (possessive), winding, several

19) My (possessive), messy, my, wrinkled, tardy (modifies **we**)

20) Few (quantitative/limiting), million (quantitative), this, new

21) next (modifies **girl**), French (proper), gold (modifies **medal**)

22) His (possessive), high-calorie (compound), secret

## Order of Adjectives

1) He bought a large green truck.

2) Few antique wooden stools are as nice as this one. (**Few** is a determiner, **antique** relates to age, and **wooden** indicates the material.)

3) I love your soft plaid blanket. (**Plaid** tells you about the design.)

4) Have you seen any narrow purple balloons? (**Any** is a determiner.)

5) The cute elderly couple made a donation to our school. (**Cute** is an opinion and **elderly** relates to age.)

6) Please hand me those white paper towels. (**Those** is a determiner and **paper** indicates the material.)

7) I ate two delicious English muffins. (**English** is an origin.)

8) Careful. These instruments have jagged metal cutting blades. (**Metal** indicates the material and **cutting** is a purpose.)

9) Would you like some spicy red peppers? (**Some** is quantitative and **spicy** is an opinion or quality.)

10) My sister plays with colorful foam building blocks. (**Foam** tells the material while **building** is a purpose.)

11) Our friendly, thoughtful neighbors baked cookies for us.
Note: **Friendly** and **thoughtful** are separated by a comma because they belong to the same category; they are both opinions.

12) Celia has three ugly Christmas sweaters. (**Christmas** is a purpose.)

## Articles

1) an onion      2) a lion      3) a watermelon

4) a yellow hat      5) an honest person      6) a huge boulder

Note: **honest** has a silent "h," whereas **huge** does not.

7) an unlit lamp      8) a unit      9) a European

Note: unit and European make the **y** sound (**unit** is pronounced YOO-NIT).

10) an eagle      11) an RF adapter      12) a U-turn

Notes: The "R" in **RF** is pronounced AR. The "U" in U-turn makes the **y** sound (**U-turn** is pronounced YOO-TURN).

## Adverbs

1) gracefully (adverb of manner; modifies the verb **skated**), across (adverb of place)

Note: Here, **across** functions as an adverb because it is not followed by a noun. Compare "We went across," where **across** functions as an adverb, with "We went across the ice," where **across** functions as a preposition. When **across** is followed by a noun (the ice), it is a preposition.

2) soon (adverb of time), Then (conjunctive adverb; indicates when they can go inside), inside (adverb of place)

Note: Inside functions as an adverb because it is not followed by a noun (like "inside the house"). See the note to Exercise 1.

3) too (intensifier), again (adverb of frequency)

4) rarely (adverb of frequency), tomorrow (adverb of time)

5) nervously (adverb of manner), above (adverb of place)

Note: Here, **above** functions as an adverb because it is not followed by a noun. Compare with "Look above your head," where **above** functions as a preposition because it is followed by a noun (your head).

6) Fortunately (conjunctive adverb), diligently (adverb of manner)

7) always (adverb of frequency), hence (adverb of reason)

Note: **unnecessary** is an adjective (not an adverb).

8) suddenly (adverb of time), too (intensifier)

9) completely (adverb of degree; intensifier), barely (adverb of degree; intensifier)

10) Where (interrogative adverb), typically (adverb of frequency), here (adverb of place)

Note: As an adverb, **here** means "in this place," while as a noun, **here** means "this place." Compare "Leave it here," which could be written "Leave it in this place," where **here** functions as an adverb, with "Let's go from here," which could be written, "Let's go from this place," where **here** functions as a noun. The word **in** makes a big difference.

11) Why (interrogative adverb), Even (adverb of degree; intensifier), well (adverb of manner; modifies the verb **work**)

Note: **everything** is a pronoun (not an adverb), unlike everywhere; **everything** does not answer why, how, how much, how often, when, where, to what degree, to what extent, or under what circumstances.

Note: **broken** is an adjective (not an adverb); **is** is a linking verb.

12) very (intensifier), therefore (conjunctive adverb), just (adverb of degree, meaning "only" in this context), briefly (adverb of time)

Note: tired is an adjective (not an adverb); **am** is a linking verb.

## Adverb vs. Adjective

1) wisely (adverb; describes how to choose)

2) costly (adjective; **was** is a form of **to be**; describes the war)

3) late (adjective; **stay** is a linking verb, as in "Will you **be** late?")

4) late (adverb; describes when the quiz started)

5) hard (adverb; describes how she worked)

6) hard (adjective; **looked** is a linking verb, as in "It **was** hard")

7) friendly (adjective; **seems** is a linking verb, as in "She **is** friendly")

8) already (adverb; this is tricky because **are** is a linking verb; however, the adverb **already** does not modify a verb in this case; recall that an adverb can modify a verb, an adjective, adverb, or a clause; **already** is an adverb of time, indicating when the guests will be here)

9) right (adjective; describes the noun **turn**; in this exercise, the adjective is an attributive adjective, not a predicate adjective)

10) right (adverb; modifies the action verb **turn**; in this exercise, **turn** is a verb, whereas **turn** was used as a noun in the previous exercise)

11) close (adverb; describes where to sit)

12) close (adjective; **is** is a form of to **be**; describes the score)

13) bad (adjective; **looks** is a linking verb, as in, "This **is** bad")

14) poorly (adverb; describes how they played)

15) badly (adverb; describes how it could go)

16) bad (adjective; **feel** is a linking verb, as in, "We **were** bad")

17) good (adjective; **are** is a form of **to be**; describes the people)

18) well (adverb; describes how you should do)

19) good (adjective; describes the noun **feeling**; in this exercise, the adjective is an attributive adjective, not a predicate adjective)

20) well (adjective; **well** is an adjective when it refers to health; **feel** is a linking verb, as in, "I **am** well today")

## Degrees

1) darker, darkest

2) more dangerous, most dangerous

3) more boring, most boring

4) healthier, healthiest

5) more dramatic, most dramatic

6) more polite, most polite

7) paler, palest

8) more tired, most tired

9) tidier, tidiest

10) thinner, thinnest

11) better, best

12) more finicky, most finicky

13) spunkier, spunkiest

14) gentler, gentlest

15) more gently, most gently      16) unfriendlier, unfriendliest

Note: Since **gently** can only be an adverb, it doesn't follow the rule for two-syllable adjectives that end in **y**.

17) My cousin's hair is smoother than mine.

18) He is the most famous actor we know.

19) The living room is dimmer than the kitchen.

20) Greg visits more frequently than Derek does.

21) That is the creamiest soup on the menu.

22) He could be the most excited puppy in the world.

23) The opening is narrower than I expected.

24) Nobody comes here more often than I do.

25) Give me the simplest explanation possible.

26) My tutor speaks more simply than my teacher.

Note: Since **simply** can only be an adverb, it doesn't follow the rule for two-syllable adjectives that end in **y**.

27) Please wake up earlier than you did today.

Note: Since **early** can function as an adjective or as an adverb, it follows the rule for two-syllable adjectives that end in **y** (regardless of whether it is used as an adjective or as an adverb). Note how this is different from Exercise 26.

28) He behaves more awkwardly than his brother.

## Prepositions

1) across, over, up

2) in, against

3) of, under, inside

4) with, during

5) in, over, of, on

6) about, after

7) through, around, into

8) For, without, down by

9) At, before, of

10) Behind, near, of

11) for, by

12) for, from, of

13) from, past

14) for, to, at

15) along, to, beyond

## Conjunctions

1) and (coordinating), but (coordinating)

2) either/or (correlative)

3) where (subordinating)

4) yet (coordinating), and (coordinating)

5) While (subordinating)

6) Both/and (correlative)

7) so (coordinating)

8) neither/nor (correlative)

9) if (subordinating), and (coordinating)

10) as if (subordinating)

11) After (subordinating), and (coordinating)

12) until (subordinating)

13) not only/but also (correlative)

## Interjections

1) Aha

2) Wow

3) well

4) Why

5) Whew

6) Oh no

7) um

8) Sh

9) Yippee

## Parts of Speech

1) Follow (verb), through (preposition; connects the nouns **path** and **forest**), forest (noun), you (pronoun)

2) became (verb), suspicious (predicate adjective; follows the linking verb **became**; modifies **mother**), when (subordinating conjunction; joins

two clauses), cheerfully (adverb of manner)

3) Who (interrogative pronoun), cracked (participial adjective; modifies **window**), amazing (adjective; modifies **job**), job (noun)

4) Oh (interjection), that (demonstrative pronoun; the preposition **of** has to take a noun or pronoun; **that** isn't used as an adjective here because it doesn't modify a noun), Your (possessive adjective; modifies **suggestion**), suggestion (noun)

5) ordered (verb), larger (comparative adjective), yet (coordinating conjunction), too (adverb of degree; modifies **small**).

6) gingerly (adverb of manner), fragile (adjective; modifies **knickknack**), knickknack (noun), inside (it mainly functions as a preposition, as it joins the nouns **knickknack** and **case**; recall the section entitled "Adverb vs. Adjective")

7) someone (indefinite pronoun), invents (verb), chores (noun), test (verb)

8) Either (correlative conjunction; part of the pair **either**/**or**), these (demonstrative pronoun; it isn't used as an adjective here because it doesn't modify a noun), by (preposition; relates the verb **altered** to the noun **noon**), new (adjective; modifies the **pair of pants**)

9) baby (noun), dropped (verb), again (adverb of frequency), Uh oh (interjection)

10) If (subordinating conjunction), set (verb), beside (preposition; connects the nouns **phone** and **wallet**), outside (adverb of place; it doesn't function as a preposition in this instance because it doesn't join a noun to another part of speech).

11) many (quantitative adjective), floor (noun), Why (interrogative adverb), his (possessive pronoun; it isn't used as an adjective here because it doesn't modify a noun)

12) Kimberly (proper noun), suddenly (adverb of time/manner), asked (verb), Where (interrogative adverb)

13) Unless (subordinating conjunction), you (personal pronoun), learn (verb), otherwise (adverb)

14) seems (linking verb), obvious (predicate adjective; follows the linking verb **seems**), um (interjection), between (preposition; relates the verb **fit** to the noun **posts**)

15) Chicago's (proper possessive noun), best (superlative adjective), tasted (verb), almost (adverb of degree; note that **good** is a predicate adjective that follows the linking verb **is**, which is a form of **to be**, and the adverb **almost** modifies the adjective **good**)

16) denied (verb), damage (noun), his (possessive adjective; modifies the noun **fault**; compare with Exercise 11), own (adjective; also modifies the noun **fault**), fault (noun)

17) fainted (verb), during (adverb of time), Spanish (proper adjective), class (noun)

## Word Usage

1) Pronoun examples: Give me a **few**. A **few** of the eggs are broken. (When using **few** as an indefinite pronoun, there should **not** be a noun immediately after **few**; however, there may be a preposition like **of** between **few** and the noun.)

Adjective example: **Few** students study as hard as she does. (The quantitative adjective **few** modifies the noun **students**.)

2) Preposition example: We flew **over** the ocean. (As a preposition, **over** takes a noun as an object. The object of **over** is **the ocean**.)

Adverb examples: The tree fell **over**. When can you come **over**? (As an adverb, **over** is not followed by a noun.)

3) Noun example: The plumber gave me an **estimate**. (The noun **estimate** is the object of the **verb** gave.)

Verb example: Please **estimate** the cost for me. (The verb **estimate** indicates the action that the plumber did.)

4) Adjective example: I am **through** with it. (As an adjective, **through** means "finished." It can follow a linking verb like **to be**, or it can be used the way it is in "through traffic." Beware that **through** functions as an adverb when it modifies an action verb, as in "He just passed through," and **through** functions as a preposition when it takes a noun as an object, as in "Drive through the tunnel.")

Preposition example: Let's walk **through** the park. (As a preposition, **through** takes a noun as an object. The object of **through** is **the park**.)

5) Conjunction example: We will play baseball **after** my arm heals. (As a subordinating conjunction, **after** joins two clauses together.)

Preposition example: I need to do my homework **after** dinner. (As a preposition, after takes a noun as an object. The object of **after** is **dinner**. Without a noun following, it would function as an adverb, as in "We'll watch a movie and talk after.")

6) Adverb example: **When** does the bus depart? (The interrogative form makes it clear that **when** functions primarily as an adverb.)

Conjunction example: **When** she looked in my direction, I smiled. (As a subordinating conjunction, **when** joins two clauses together. One could also write, "I smiled when she looked in my direction," though the opposite order makes it easy to identify the two separate clauses.)

7) Preposition example: We have been waiting since the morning. (As a preposition, **since** takes a noun as an object. The object of **since** is **the morning**. Beware that **since** can also be used as an adverb, as in, "I arrived at noon and have been here since.")

Conjunction example: Since you are sick today, I will return tomorrow. (As a subordinating conjunction, **since** joins two clauses together.)

8) Adverb example: You did well. (Beware that **well** functions as an adjective when it refers to health condition or wellness, as in, "I feel

well today.")

Interjection example: Well, let's go.

## Capitalization

1) My, Devon Carter, He, Wichita, Kansas

2) This, It, Friday (don't capitalize **yesterday**)

3) Our, Spanish, Statue of Liberty (don't capitalize **summer**)

4) On, Veteran's Day, I (don't capitalize **general**; no name is included)

5) He, General Grant (here the title includes the name), Mr. Dean's

6) Buy, Wal-Mart (alternative common spelling is Walmart), Crest (don't capitalize **soap**; an incomplete sentence follows the colon)

7) She, Hi, Dad (used as a name), Could

8) Where, Nike, My, Amazon (don't capitalize **dad**; not used as a name)

9) Have, *The Prince and the Pauper*, Mark Twain

10) My, Travel, Whittier Boulevard (**aunt** is not used as a name)

Note: **west** is **not** capitalized here because it simply refers to direction. Compare "drive to the west" with "a cowboy from the Old West."

11) Back, Uncle Danny (**uncle** is used with a name).

Note: Don't capitalize this quote because it is not a complete sentence (in contrast to Exercise 10).

12) This, Easter, March, April (don't capitalize **it**)

Note: Don't capitalize a word following a semicolon, regardless of whether or not a complete thought follows the semicolon (the rule for capitalizing complete sentences that follow a colon does not apply to semicolons).

13) My, English, French, Latin (don't capitalize **dad**; not used as a name)

Note: Since English is a proper adjective, it is capitalized even though an incomplete sentence follows the colon.

## End Punctuation

1) It was foggy this morning.  
2) What is your favorite color?  
3) Are you ready for the quiz?  
4) "I won!" he exclaimed.  
5) Stop! Give it back now!  
6) I forgot. Do you know it?  

Note: In Exercise 5, the exclamation marks assume that the speaker is conveying strong emotion. If this was said without strong emotion, then periods would be appropriate.

7) I'm not sure about this.  
8) "Get out!" she screamed.  
9) When he arrives, let me know.  
10) How are you? I'm fine.  

## Abbreviations

1) Last spring, they went on a field trip to Houston, **TX**.

Note: **TX** is the current two-letter postal abbreviation for **Texas**. Past abbreviations include **TEX** and **Tex.**

2) My dental **appt.** is on **Oct.** 24.

3) Our **ETA** is 7:15 **a.m.**

Note: **a.m.** stands for "ante meridiem," which means "before noon." Depending on the context, it may also be written as **AM** or **A.M.**

4) Today we will visit with **VP** Chan.

Note: **Vice-President** is sometimes abbreviated as **V.P.**

5) We won a trip to visit Washington, **D.C.**!

6) His full name is Frank Henry Cavendish, **Jr.**

7) Does **Mrs.** Valdez still live at 135 **E.** Seventh **Ave.**?

## Commas

1) Yes, your uncle was born in Miami, Florida, on September 16, 1984.

2) We have tickets to tonight's play, and it begins in less than an hour.

3) To her surprise, the dishes, bowls, and cups had been washed and dried. Note: The comma after **bowls** is considered optional.

4) The baby looked at the familiar woman who approached, and clapped. Note: This comma shows that the baby clapped, not the woman.

5) Ready or not, we will be leaving in an hour to pick up Alan Pratt Sr. Note: No comma is needed before Jr. or Sr.

6) Do you, Charles, know where Leonard was on Friday, May 7, 2021?

7) Since Amy must be hungry, offer her some angel food cake and punch.

8) Her suggestion, which proved to be helpful, was to find a new tutor.

9) For the second time, any medicine that has expired should be discarded. Note: Many writers use the relative pronoun **which** for non-essential groups of words (with commas) and the relative pronoun **that** for essential groups of words (without commas). Here, "that has expired" is an essential group of words because if these words are removed, what remains is "any medicine should be discarded."

10) A large brown bear weighs 1500 lbs., which is heavier than a golf cart. Notes: For scientific measurements, a comma is common when the value exceeds 10,000. These adjectives are not reversible (so no comma comes between them), as "brown large bear" would sound funny.

11) Kim Park, Ph.D., is a knowledgeable, experienced professor of physics. Note: It could alternatively say "an experienced, knowledgeable professor," as these adjectives are reversible.

12) Our boss wants an inventory of nails, bolts, nuts, etc., by next week.

13) The boy said, "Mom wants to know where you are, Dad."

14) Grandma, my coach called me a "quick learner" during practice. Note: "quick learner" is not a complete thought.

15) She claimed to have been cleaning all day, yet the house was messy.

16) Vacuum, mop the floors, and do the laundry when you get home. Note: The comma after **floors** is considered optional.

17) When the printer runs out of ink, replace the toner cartridge.

18) Hannah, Leslie, and I played miniature golf and went swimming.

Note: The comma after **Leslie** is considered optional.

19) Freezing from the snow, they lit the fireplace as soon as they entered.

20) Trailing behind them was the mayor, Howard Madison III.

21) Well, we could visit on May 23, 2023, July 9, 2023, or March 18, 2024. Note: The comma before **or** is considered optional.

22) "The movie we saw," he said, "was surprisingly charming and witty." Note: **surprisingly** modifies both **charming** and **witty**.

23) Their only son, Bart, discovered fossils dated 8000 BC and 24,000 BC. Notes: Years use a comma when they have more than four digits. Since Bart is their only son, this information is non-essential, so commas are used.

24) My cousin Erica was born in Tulsa, OK. She is my favorite cousin. Note: **Erica** is essential information to clarify which cousin, so no comma is used. Compare with Exercise 23.

25) Ah, that first sip is quite refreshing after a few hours of hard work.

26) With his main competitor out of the race, he started to relax a little.

27) The man with the long hair and beard came here from Tokyo, Japan.

28) Put your stinky, sweaty socks in the hamper, not on the couch. Note: It could alternatively say "sweaty, stinky socks," as these adjectives are reversible.

29) My brother left his brown teddy bear on the dining table, I think. Note: These adjectives are not reversible (so no comma comes between them), as **teddy bear** functions as a single unit.

30) The child pulling the wagon is the daughter of Marcus Watts, M.D. Note: "pulling the wagon" is essential (so no commas are used) to indicate which child is the daughter.

31) Tying her hair in a pony tail, she said, "I'm ready to play."

32) His only book, *Mayflower*, was published on Thanksgiving 1978.

Notes: **No** comma is used in day-year format. Since *Mayflower* is the author's only book, this is non-essential (so commas are used).

33) Her book *Not Real* was published on April 14, 2021. It was her best.

Note: "It was her best" indicates that she wrote more than one book, so the title is essential to indicate which book (so no commas are used).

34) Shannon, Theresa, and I will be in the same class next year, I hope.

Note: The comma after **Theresa** is considered optional.

35) Delighted that the package had arrived, she raced down the stairs.

36) With her face covered in chocolate, she claimed, "I didn't eat them."

37) Mom, did Dad really say that "taxes are the cruelest thing ever"?

Note: Since the quote follows the conjunction **that**, no comma is used.

38) That tractor, though it is rusty and dented, still gets the job done.

## Colon vs. Semicolon

1) She painted the picture using three colors: blue, black, and yellow.

Note: The comma after **black** is considered optional.

2) I need to change my tie; I spilled coffee on this one.

3) Let's go to the library; it's a quiet place to study.

4) He always hides his snack in the same place: a box under his bed.

5) The omelet was cooked to perfection: fluffy with melted cheese.

Tip: In Exercises 2-3, the semicolon divides the sentence into two complete thoughts; this is characteristic of a semicolon. In Exercises 4–5, the colon divides the sentence into one complete thought and one incomplete thought; this is common, although it is possible for a colon to divide a sentence into two complete thoughts similar to a semicolon (that's where things can get a little trickier; in those cases, the distinction is that the clause before the colon introduces the clause that follows the colon).

6) It is already 7:45 a.m.; you are running late for school.

7) The old saying proved to be true: "What goes around comes around."

8) My uncle has two left feet; that is, he is a clumsy dancer.

9) These are thoughts I strive to live by: Be kind. Be positive. Be happy.

10) Let me ask you this: If you could have a superpower, what would it be?

11) Has your sister read *Pinkalicious: Tickled Pink* by Victoria Kann?

12) Victor is recovering from a hamstring injury; otherwise, he would be running in the marathon.

13) My brother eats an unusual combination of foods at the same time for a snack: celery and rice cakes.

14) I used the internet to take virtual tours of the following places: Moscow, Russia; England; Paris, France; Italy; and Cairo, Egypt. Note: Moscow, Paris, and Cairo are cities in Russia, France, and Egypt, respectively, whereas no cities were given for England or Italy.

15) Kyle is waiting for his mother to pick him up; he has been waiting here since 3:15 p.m.

16) He wrote a story entirely out of clichés; for example, it begins with the following line: "Once upon a time, it was a dark and stormy night."

17) We watched *Spider-Man: No Way Home*; we thought that the movie was good, but we liked *Spider-Man: Homecoming* better.

18) Follow these directions: Preheat the oven to 375 degrees. Place the pizza on a cookie sheet. Cook for 18 to 21 minutes.

19) That goat will eat almost anything; for instance, one time when I was cleaning his pen, he started to chew my pant leg.

20) I earned the following grades this semester: B's in language arts, physical science, and social studies; A's in algebra, computer science, and physical education; and C's in graphic arts and college prep.

21) The car is low on gas; therefore, we will need to stop at the gas station on the way home.

22) Maybe Andrew would sign up for summer camp; besides, he had

been wanting to learn how to swim.

23) The highest US population totals in 2020 were 8,804,190 in New York, NY; 3,898,747 in Los Angeles, CA; 2,746,388 in Chicago, IL; 2,304,580 in Houston, TX; and 1,608,139 in Phoenix, AZ.

Note: **No** colon precedes this list because "The highest US population totals in 2020 were" is not a complete thought.

## Apostrophes

1) The students didn't know when Abraham Lincoln's birthday was.

2) We'll visit Nguyen's mother's neighbors on the way back.

3) That shirt's pattern is dull. Of all the shirts, why'd he buy that one?

4) He's upset that Cassie's new puppy doesn't seem to like him.

5) Fixing Dad's computer shouldn't take long. I'll be there soon.

6) We haven't done much yet. You've done much more than we have.

7) His friend's sister said, "These aren't my slippers. They're hers."

8) She'd packed the children's clothes days before the vacation began.

9) Chris's clock wasn't working this morning. That's why he's late today.

10) We're driving past the Klines' house now. They are nice neighbors.

Note: **Klines'** is a plural possessive. Multiple Klines live at that house.

11) Don't worry; there are three M.D.'s in this room.

12) You know that you're not allowed in the gym without your gym shoes.

13) Not one of the library's books had the information that he wanted.

14) Let's choose the teams. The referee will now hide both teams' tokens.

Note: There are two teams and each team has tokens, so **teams'** is a plural possessive.

15) I'll stay at Nicholas' house this weekend. His parents invited me.

Note: A three-syllable proper noun ending with **s** has one apostrophe in its possessive form (without an additional **s**). It is **Nicholas'**, not **Nicholas's**.

16) I still have time to dot my i's and cross my t's before I turn it in.

17) It's surprising that the company lost all of its contracts this year.

Note: **It's** is a contraction for "It is," whereas **its** is a possessive pronoun.

18) Who's responsible for washing the skyscraper's windows?

Note: Assuming that the question is only referring to a single skyscraper, then **skyscraper's** is correct. (If the person were instead asking about the windows of multiple skyscrapers, then it would be **skyscrapers' windows**.)

## Contractions

1) had not

2) you will

3) she is/has

4) will not

5) they are

6) let us

7) I am

8) could have

9) it is (old poetic)

10) we had/would/should

11) you all (informal, southern)

12) madam (informal)

13) who have

14) until (informal)

15) it was (old poetic)

16) international

## Quotation Marks

1) Ms. Hathaway said, "The final exam counts for ten percent of the final grade and covers material from throughout the semester."

2) The refund policy states, "Merchandise may be returned for a refund or exchange within 30 days with a receipt of purchase."

3) "Professor," asked Simon, "what does the word 'doohickey' mean? Is that a particular kind of device?"

Note: It is **not** necessary to capitalize **what** because it continues from the previous part: "Professor, what does the word 'doohickey' mean?"

4) We recently read the poem "Jabberwocky" by Lewis Carroll in *A Treasury of Favorite Poems*.

5) The booklet states, "The wand will glow for up to eight hours." To summarize the rest, it says that we should avoid contact with skin.

Note: The second sentence offers a summary; these aren't the **exact** words from the booklet, so no quotation marks are used.

6) "We are glad that all of you came," said the host, "to help us celebrate the graduation of our twin sons, Jerry and Jose."

7) Naomi wrote a short story called "Looking without Seeing"; it is much different from her first short story, "Seemingly Endless."

Note: Semicolons and colons go **outside**; comms and periods go **inside**.

8) The child kept repeating the words "dry mouth" until her mother handed her a bottle of juice.

9) Kids screamed that a spider was in the house. The father yelled, "Stop shouting!" When it was quiet, the father escorted the spider outside.

Notes: The word **that** in the first sentence suggests that "a spider was in the house" were not the exact words of the kids, so no quotation marks are used there. The exclamation mark goes inside of the quotation marks in this case because **Stop shouting!** is an exclamation.

10) My mom only likes two songs better than Selena Gomez's "Rare": "Shake it Off" by Taylor Swift and "Better Be Good to Me" by Tina Turner. Note: A colon comes after an end quotation mark.

11) The teacher asked, "What are the last four words of 'The Star-Spangled Banner'?" Is the answer "home of the brave"?

Notes: Since the first double quote is a question, a question mark comes before the end double quote (but it comes after the end single quote because the song title is not a question). Since the second double quote is not a question, this question mark comes after the end double quote.

12) Quit singing the song "Grandma Got Run Over by a Reindeer"! That song is starting to get on my nerves.

Note: Since the title of the song is **not** an exclamation, the exclamation mark comes after the end quotation mark.

13) "Did you see the helicopter on the roof of the building?" she asked. That helicopter is Mr. Williams'.

Notes: The quotation is a question, so the question mark comes before the end quotation mark. The apostrophe is part of the possessive noun, Williams', so it comes before the period (it is not a single quotation mark).

14) "We're trying to see," he said, "how many words we can form using letters in the word 'language.'"

Note: The end single and end double quotation marks both come after the period. Contrast this with the apostrophe in Exercise 13.

15) Becca said, "Can I eat the soup now? I'm starving."

Her mother replied, "It's very hot. Wait for it to cool down."

"Please let me try. I'll be careful."

"Okay. But remember that I warned you."

## Hyphens

1) Nathan's sister-in-law is friends with Collin's daughter-in-law.

2) One student answered forty-eight out of fifty questions correctly.

3) Please give this yo-yo to the boy wearing the blue T-shirt.

4) Your photo will look nicer if you apply the red-eye filter.

5) The phone number 555-1212 is used in movies and television shows.

6) It was unlike any other fourteenth-century painting she had seen.

7) Three-fourths of the patients never had an X-ray taken before.

8) His parents signed him up for a top-notch golf academy.

9) "My name is Marcous," the boy said. "It's spelled M-a-r-c-o-u-s."

10) The combination to the locker is 18-31-15.

## Compound Words

1) teacup

2) pet food

3) one-sided

4) healthcare

5) pencil cup

6) part-time

7) overnight

8) leap year

9) runner-up

10) guardrail

11) sea salt

12) high-rise

13) four-wheel drive

14) whatsoever

15) football stadium

16) tri-state area

## Phrasal Adjectives

1) The spacious closet included a full-length mirror.

2) Biographies can be found in the second-to-last aisle.

3) My brother finished the race second to last. Note: Hyphens are unnecessary when a phrasal adjective comes after a noun.

4) The forecast calls for partly cloudy skies over the weekend.

5) I am twenty-nine years old. Have you met my three-year-old son?

6) Stephanie proved to be a very sweet girl.

7) All we have left is a half-eaten sandwich.

8) The ceiling is twelve feet high. I need my eight-foot ladder.

Notes: **twelve feet** comes after **ceiling**; **eight-foot** comes before **ladder**.

9) We really like the hands-free faucet in the bathroom.

10) This is the delightful, charming neighbor I was telling you about.

Notes: **delightful** and **charming** are two separate adjectives (they do not form one thought), so **no** hyphen is used. A comma separates them because they are reversible (it could alternatively say "charming, delightful neighbor").

11) The manager was fond of the new employee's can-do attitude.

12) It's the twenty-first century, yet he has a horse-drawn carriage.

13) Nobody will believe his story about the little green men.

Notes: **little** and **green** are two separate adjectives (they do not form one thought), so **no** hyphen is used. **No** comma separates them because the order can't be reversed (since "green little men" doesn't sound right).

14) Here is an up-to-date list of dentists in our state.

15) Our records are always up to date.

Note: Unlike Exercise 14, here **up to date** comes after the noun.

16) They call it a five-star neighborhood, but I would give it three stars.

17) It was a once-in-a-lifetime opportunity.

## Word Division

1) frac-tion

2) de-cent

3) blan-ket

4) zip-per

5) so-cial

6) trained

Note: the **ia** of social make a single vowel sound (a soft "uh").

Note: **trained** may **not** be divided because it is a one-syllable word.

7) hum-ble

8) eye-brow

9) bat-tle

10) sur-geon

11) pre-cise

12) fig-ure

13) ocean

14) base-ment

Note: Avoid dividing **ocean** because its first syllable (**o**) has one letter.

15) farm-ing

16) win-ning

Note: An **ing** suffix usually doesn't break up a root. Hence, the syllables of **farming** are farm-ing (**not** far-ming). The doubled **n** in **winning** allows the **ing** to connect with an **n** without breaking up the root **win**.

17) tri-fle

18) trib-ute

Note: Contrast the open syllable **tri** with a long **i** in **trifle** with the closed syllable **trib** with a short **i** in **tribute**.

19) joy-ous

20) tai-lor

21) pleas-ant

22) re-ac-tion

23) al-ter-nate

24) lone-li-ness

Note: **alternate** divides the same whether it is used as an adjective, noun, or verb (even though it is pronounced differently as a verb).

25) se-ri-ous                              26) op-po-site

Note: **serious** divides as se-ri-ous even though it is often pronounced sir-ee-us. This is a rare exception of division versus pronunciation.

27) con-cern-ing                           28) inter-twine

Note: An **ing** suffix usually doesn't break up a root. Hence, the syllables of **concerning** are con-cern-ing (**not** con-cer-ning).

Note: The preferred division of **intertwine** is the natural inter-twine, even though it has three syllables (in/ter/twine).

29) maga-zine                              30) tem-pera-ture

Note: Although **magazine** is pronounced with three syllables (mag/a/zine), since the middle syllable has one letter (**a**), it is preferable to divide it as maga-zine (instead of mag-azine). It is similarly undesirable to break **temperature** before the **a** (as temper-ature).

31) fa-cili-tate                           32) un-be-liev-able

Note: Similar to the notes to Exercises 29–30, it is undesirable to break **facilitate** before the **i** (as facil-itate).

Note: In contrast to Exercises 29–31, it is undesirable to break **unbelievable** after the **a** (rather than before it) because the ending **able** is more natural than the ending **ble**.

## Dashes

1) When she went to the museum with her friends last week, the strangest thing happened—just a minute, I need to take this phone call.

2) Two of our cats—the striped one and the gray one—woke me up last night because they had gotten locked in my room.

3) I still need to grab my things—have you seen my passport?—before we drive to the airport.

4) "Let's see," he said. "You owe me five—no, it's actually seven—dollars for your supplies."

5) "The girl reading the newspaper"—she lowered her voice to a whisper—"knows everyone at the school. You should ask her."

Note: The dashes appear outside of the quotation because the narrator (not the speaker) is interrupting the statement.

6) We're cycling past the dump—ew, that odor is disgusting!—right now on our way to the theater.

## Parentheses

1) Michelangelo (1475-1564) is famous for his Renaissance artwork.

2) Read about metaphors (pp. 163-178) before our next class.

3) My sister is a huge fan of horror (don't ask me why) novels and movies.

4) It sounds like it will be fun (too bad I have to work tomorrow).

5) She doesn't even know that I exist. (Sigh.)

Notes: In Exercise 5, the period goes inside of the parentheses because the entire (one-word) sentence is enclosed in parentheses. In contrast, in Exercise 4, the period goes outside of the parentheses because only part of the sentence is enclosed in parentheses.

6) Paint was peeling (inside and outside), so I hired a handyman.

7) Does anyone know what we're supposed to do (because I don't)?

8) You love teaching (don't you?) and we have a lecturer position to fill.

Notes: In Exercise 8, the question mark is inside of the parentheses because the text in parentheses asks a question. In contrast, in Exercise 7, the question mark is outside of parentheses because the text outside (not inside) asks the question.

9) "The author [Sheena Patel] is currently working on her third novel."

10) Her lab was donated by one of our alumni (J.D. Farr [1938–2017]).

## Ellipsis Points

1) I visited . . . Vermont last week.

2) The radio . . . stopped working.

3) She . . . won a bronze medal.

4) The cat . . . broke a vase.

5) He said . . . that it won't matter.

6) We played cards. . . . It was fun. Note: There are four dots.

## Italics

1) Our teacher asked us to read the chapter called "Periodic Properties of the Elements" in the book entitled *Chemistry: The Central Science*.

2) Posted on his wall was an article with the headline "Berlin Wall Tumbles" from the *London Herald* newspaper.

3) "This woman is looking for her *welpe*," said the girl. "From her gestures, I think it means that she lost her puppy."

4) Do you know if the book *A Treasury of Favorite Poems* includes the poem "A Dream Within a Dream" by Edgar Allen Poe?

5) *Titanic*, *Pride & Prejudice*, and *Bridget Jones's Diary* are three of my mother's favorite movies.

6) Do you know the distinction between the words *predicament*, *dilemma*, and *quandary*? Note: Quotation marks would be fine instead.

7) I read the article "Why movies need the big screen" in *Time* magazine (Vol. 192, Nos. 19-20).

8) When the man saw the shiny red sports car pass by, he exclaimed, "*Mamma mia!* Now that's a fancy ride!"

9) Rembrandt's famous painting *The Night Watch* (1642) sold for over 70 million dollars in 1998.

10) My little brother loves watching *Shaun the Sheep*'s thirtieth episode from the second season, which is entitled "The Big Chase."

11) In 1620, the *Mayflower* sailed from England to America with over one hundred passengers.

12) Keegan was dancing along to the song "No Judgement" from the album *Heartbreak Weather* by Niall Horan.

## Subject vs. Predicate

1) Richard/passed

2) water/dripped

3) It/was

4) pair (of shoes)/remained

5) suit and tie/were

6) Dr. Sasha Malovic/prescribed

7) car/made and shook

8) He/tiptoed

9) nobody/is

10) Mr. and Mrs. Hope/ate and watched

11) you (implied)/follow and use

Note: **advice** and **sense** are the direct objects of the verbs, **not** the subject. The person who is being spoken to (you) is the person who may follow the advice or who may use common sense.

12) Maria, Nicole, and Riley/collided

13) flock (of birds)/came

Note: This sentence has an inverted structure. Instead of the usual order (subject then verb), this sentence is inverted to give the verb first. It could alternatively read, "A flock of birds came out of the fog." In this form, it is easy to see that **flock (of birds)** is the simple subject.

14) you (implied)/Invite

Note: **friends** are part of the prepositional phrase "of your friends," **not** the subject. The person who is being spoken to (you) is the person who will invite them. It is instructive to compare this exercise with the previous exercise. This exercise doesn't have an inverted order; you can't rewrite it so that the friends do the inviting (without destroying the meaning and intent of the sentence).

## Complements

1) window (direct object)

2) kid (indirect object), ball (direct object)

Notes: You can rewrite this as "He handed a ball **to** the kid"; **ball** is the direct object because the ball is what was handed.

3) mine (predicate nominative; **mine** is a pronoun; **is** is a form of **to be**)

4) blue (predicate adjective; **are** is a form of **to be**)

5) flower (direct object), pink (object complement)

6) it (direct object)

7) rowdy (predicate adjective; **became** is a linking verb)

8) man (direct object), tired (object complement)

9) Heidi (direct object)

10) me (direct object)

11) hamster (direct object), Hammy (object complement)

12) her (indirect object), news (direct object)

Notes: You can rewrite this as "Tell the news **to** her"; **news** is the direct object because the news is what will be told.

13) book (direct object)

14) friend (direct object), Mason (object complement)

15) hair (direct object), short (object complement)

16) cheering (predicate adjective; **were** is a form of **to be**; **cheering** is a participial adjective)

17) me (indirect object), phone (direct object)

Notes: You can rewrite this as "Please hand the phone **to** me"; **phone** is the direct object because the phone is what will be handed (over).

18) bills (direct object)

19) fun (predicate adjective; **sounded** is a linking verb because it could be replaced with a form of **to be**: "The game **was** fun")

20) cookware (direct object)

21) socks (direct object)

22) us (direct object)

23) broken (predicate adjective; **is** is a form of **to be**; **broken** is a participial adjective)

24) Wade (indirect object), towel (direct object)

Notes: You can rewrite this as "Give a towel **to** Wade"; **towel** is the direct object because the towel is what will be given.

## Phrases

1) Example: This book is about astronomy. Note: To function as an adjective, the phrase needs to describe a noun. In this example, it functions as a predicate adjective that describes the noun **book**.

2) Example: Put the ice-cream in the freezer. Note: To function as an adverb, the phrase needs to describe a verb, an adjective, or another adverb. In this example, it functions as an adverb of place.

3) Example: Wash the dirty laundry today. Note: If you use the phrase as the subject of the sentence, the object of a (non-linking) transitive verb, or the object of a preposition, it will function as a noun. In this example, it is the object of the verb **Wash**.

4) Example: I would be feeling better if I could get some rest.

5) Example: Yvette is studying for the test. Note: To function as an adjective, the phrase needs to describe a noun. In this example, it functions as a predicate adjective that describes the noun **Yvette**.

6) Example: You can get a better grade by studying for the test. Notes: If

you use the phrase as the subject of the sentence, the object of a (non-linking) transitive verb, or the object of a preposition, it will function as a noun. In this example, it is the object of the preposition **by**. If you attempt to use it as the object of a verb, make sure that the verb is **not** a linking verb (otherwise, it may be used as a predicate adjective).

7) Example: My sister loves to eat fruit. Notes: Compare this example with "My sister loves jewelry." This example shows how to use the phrase as the object of a transitive verb (that isn't a linking verb). It may help to review the section entitled "Infinitives."

8) Example: Lionel, a man on a mission, ignored all of the bystanders.

## Clauses

1) unless we raise more money (adverb; gives a condition)

2) because it was a size too small (adverb of reason)

3) whose dog is loose (adjective; describes the noun **person**)

4) While they waited in line (adverb of time)

5) if you are trying to avoid dairy products (adverb; gives a condition)

6) what you did (noun; object of the verb **know**)

7) where people are friendly (adverb of place)

8) What she wants (noun; subject of the sentence)

9) When the repairman arrives (adverb of time)

10) that you gave me (adjective; describes the noun **golf balls**)

11) so that their dog couldn't escape (adverb of reason)

12) which the city plans to build (adjective; describes the noun **stadium**; here, **which** is similar in usage to that in Exercise 10, except in this exercise **which** is nonrestrictive whereas in Exercise 10 **that** is restrictive)

## Types of Sentences

1) Interrogative

2) Declarative

3) Exclamatory

4) Imperative

5) Declarative

6) Interrogative

7) Imperative

8) Exclamatory

9) Interrogative

10) Imperative

11) Declarative

12) Imperative

13) Exclamatory

14) Interrogative

## Sentence Structures

1) simple (one independent clause, no dependent clauses)

2) complex (**If** functions as a subordinating conjunction)

3) compound (**but** functions as a coordinating conjunction)

4) compound-complex (**when** functions as a subordinating conjunction)

5) simple (here, **and** simply joins two nouns together; it doesn't join two independent clauses together)

6) compound (three independent clauses joined by the coordinating conjunction **and**; note that "Eileen sang" and "Tam danced" each meet the definition of an independent clause, since each has a subject, each has a verb, and each forms a complete thought)

7) complex (**because** functions as a subordinating conjunction)

8) compound-complex (**unless** functions as a subordinating conjunction)

## Fragment vs. Run-on

1) complete sentence (subject, predicate, and complete thought)

2) fragment (what was put and where was it put?)

3) run-on (two independent clauses joined incorrectly)

4) fragment (no subject; who grabbed the man?)

5) fragment (**Although** is a subordinating conjunction)

6) run-on (multiple **and**'s join independent clauses)

7) fragment (it would make more sense to say "were spread")

8) complete sentence (a comma joins a dependent clause beginning with the subordinating conjunction **since** to an independent clause)

9) fragment (no verb)

10) fragment (the preposition **by** needs an object)

11) run-on (two independent clauses joined incorrectly)

12) complete sentence (imperative; the subject is implied)

13) run-on (two independent clauses joined incorrectly; one way to fix this would be to insert the word **but**; it's a run-on rather than a fragment because it includes two independent clauses)

## Subject-verb Agreement

1) They **were** happy when it **was** clear and sunny.

2) I **think** that the tie with the stars **goes** best with that suit.

Note: Ignore the phrase **with the stars** to get "the tie goes best."

3) Please **do** not worry; he **knows** what I **am** doing.

Note: The subject **you** is implied for the verb **do**.

4) They **have** gone fishing every time that he **has** come over.

5) My friends and I **are** skating today. Note: **My friends and I** is a compound subject.

6) She **says** to please wait for her; she **will** be here soon.

7) Either a waffle or a pancake **is** fine; both **are** delicious.

Notes: In the first clause, since two singular subjects are joined by **or**, the verb is singular. The pronoun **both** is plural.

8) Nothing **gets** done when nobody **wants** to work.

9) One stack of papers **is** on your desk, and more **are** on the way.

10) Bacon, lettuce, and tomato **is** the sandwich of the day.

Note: A bacon, lettuce, and tomato sandwich is one kind of sandwich.

11) None of us **were** ready; all of the test **was** difficult.

Note: The pronouns **None** and **all** are exceptions to the preposition rule.

12) I **forget** whether science or mathematics **is** her major.

Note: **Mathematics** is a single subject; she has a single major.

13) He will **give** us directions to the store when he **calls**.

Note: Don't add **s** to the future tense for third person singular.

14) Many of the guests **are** here. Most of the salsa **is** gone.

Note: The pronoun **most** is an exception to the prepositional phrase rule.

15) The team from the north **has** won every game this season.

Note: **Team** acts as a single unit.

16) Forty miles of desert sand **lies** between the two cities.

Note: **Forty miles** acts as a single distance.

17) The couple **has** two kids. Note: **couple** acts as a single unit.

18) Half of the fruit **was** left. A third of the nuts **were** rotten.

Note: Fractional amounts are exceptions to the prepositional phrase rule.

## Mood

1) imperative (requests action)

2) indicative (states a fact)

3) indicative (states a fact)

4) subjunctive (contrary to fact using **were** instead of **was**)

5) indicative (states a fact)

6) imperative (requests action)

7) subjunctive (contrary to fact using **were** instead of **was**)

8) indicative (states an opinion as if it were a fact)

9) indicative (states a fact)

10) imperative (requests avoiding an action)

11) indicative (states a fact)

12) subjunctive (contrary to fact using **were** instead of **was**; hypothetical)

13) imperative (requests action)

14) indicative (states a fact)

15) subjunctive (makes a request using **be** instead of **is**)

## Voice

1) His father patted him on the back.

Note: Other variations of these answers may also be correct.

2) Lightning struck the tree.

3) The teacher assigned seats to the students.

Note: The subject **teacher** was implied in the original sentence.

4) I am writing my essay. Note: The subject **I** was implied.

5) A homeless man stole Gina's purse.

6) The detective found the purse.

7) Every day, many people throw coins into the pond.

Note: The subject **people** was implied.

8) We will consider your suggestion. Note: The subject **We** was implied.

## Pronoun Mistakes

1) **We** gave Sylvia a bracelet on **her** birthday.

2) Jason and **I** went to the show. They gave **us** free goggles.

Note: **Jason and I** are subjects. You would say "I went to the show." You wouldn't say "Me went to the show."

3) Dad brought **my** friends and **me** to the park. Note: **my friends and me** are objects of the transitive verb **brought**. You would say "Dad brought me to the park." You wouldn't say "Dad brought I to the park."

4) **She** lost **her** ring last month. **She** found **it** today.

5) Mr. Ferguson shook **his** head in disbelief. Note: If this person goes by "Mr.," the masculine possessive adjective **his** should be appropriate.

6) **Who** called when **I** was in the bathroom? Note: **Who** is the subject. You might answer, "He called when I was in the bathroom." You wouldn't answer, "Him called when I was in the bathroom."

7) With **whom** did **you** dance? Note: **whom** is the object of the preposition **With**. You might answer, "I danced with him" (or "her").

You wouldn't answer, "I danced with he" (or "she").

8) Adam's grandmother left **her** dentures on the counter. (If they happen to be Adam's dentures, and not his grandmother's dentures, in that case the pronoun **him** would be correct.)

9) **I** found grapes in the refrigerator; **I** ate all of **them**.

10) **That** seat is **mine**. Please find **your** own.

11) **Whoever** figured that out is a genius. Note: **Whoever** is the subject. You might answer, "She figured that out." You wouldn't answer, "Her figured that out."

## Modifier Mistakes

1) The kid was **almost** tall enough to ride the roller coaster.

Note: There may be other satisfactory ways to rewrite the sentences.

2) Jared's boss told him he could visit the doctor **in the morning**.

3) **Starving after chopping firewood**, he ordered pizza.

4) A man **with a mustache** was riding a bicycle.

5) **While eating dinner**, Dawn asked her brother why he climbed the tree.

6) A boy **in jeans and a t-shirt** was riding a skateboard.

7) Lydia **barely** remembered to turn in her homework assignment.

8) **Singing in the shower**, the man made it hard for everyone else to concentrate.

9) **Before work**, her boss said she would be evaluated. Alternate answer: Her boss said she would be evaluated **before work**. (Without more information, there is no way to determine which meaning was intended.)

## Common Word Mix-ups

1) According to **your** watch, **it's** currently a quarter **past** four.

Notes: "According to you are watch" wouldn't make sense. "It is currently a quarter past four" does make sense. Here, **passed** would be incorrect because a verb doesn't work between quarter and four; **past** works to mean that the time is beyond four.

2) **Who's** tapping the desk? **It's** really **affecting** my concentration. Notes: "Who is tapping the desk?" makes sense. "It is really affecting my concentration" also makes sense. Here, **affecting** is a verb that indicates a change in a person's concentration.

3) The **principal** presented awards **to** students who performed very **well** in **their** courses. Notes: The **principal** is in charge of the school. The preposition **to** takes the noun **students** as an object. The adverb **well** modifies the verb **performed**. "In they are courses" wouldn't make sense; "in their courses" indicates that the courses are the students' courses.

4) **There** was no **good** reason for there to be **fewer** nurses working at the hospital this year. Notes: "They are was no good reason" wouldn't makes sense. The adjective **good** modifies the noun **reason**. Use **fewer** (not **less**) to agree with the plural **nurses**.

5) She was **accepted** into **two** different summer programs that introduce the **principles** of coding. Notes: Use **accepted** (not **excepted**) because she was included in (not excluded from) the program. The number **two** indicates how many programs there were. Here, **principles** refer to the ideas involved in coding.

6) **Their** sad stories about the hardships they faced while growing up really **affected** me, **too**. Notes: "They are sad stories" wouldn't make sense in this sentence; "their sad stories" indicates that the stories are about them. Here, **affected** is a verb that indicates a change (mental or emotional), and **too** means "also."

7) You must choose **between** Cameron and Brady; **they're** the only **two** players remaining. Notes: Use **between** for two people. "They are the only two players remaining" makes sense. The number **two** indicates how many players are left.

8) With **whom** did you go **to** the dance? It seems like everyone went

**except** for me. Notes: Use **whom** because the preposition **with** takes an object (not a subject). One might answer, "I went to the dance with him," not "with he." The preposition **to** takes the noun **dance** as an object. Use **except** (not **accept**) because someone is excluded.

9) They already **accepted their** invitations to the birthday party. **It's too** late to change the date. Notes: Use **accepted** (not **excepted**) because they were invited to (not excluded from) the party. "They already accepted they are invitations" wouldn't make sense; **their** indicates that the invitations belong to them. "It is too late" makes sense. Here, **too** acts as an intensifier.

10) One side **effect** of the medicine was that she had **less** energy than usual. Notes: Use **effect** (not **affect**) as a noun to indicate a result. Use **less** (not **fewer**) to agree with the singular **energy**.

11) **Who passed** you just before the race ended? I would like to watch the **two** of you race again. Notes: **Who** is the subject of the question (not the object of a transitive verb or a preposition). One might answer, "He passed me," not "Him passed me." Use **passed** (not **past**) because a verb is needed here; one person went ahead of another. Here, **two** indicates a specific number.

12) "**You're** responsible for dividing the chores **among** yourselves," the father said **to** his three children.
Notes: "You are responsible" makes sense. Use **among** for three (or more) people. The preposition **to** takes the noun **children** as an object.

13) **Whose** turn is it to **lie** down on the hammock? My brother would like a turn, **too**. Notes: "Whose turn" indicates a sense of belonging; "Who is turn is it" wouldn't make sense. Use **lie** to mean "to rest" without an object (**down** isn't an object here because it functions as an adverb in this sentence). Here, **too** means "also."

14) **Lay** the rug in the middle of the living room for now. We can adjust

**its** position later. Notes: Use **lay** to mean "to place" with **rug** as an object. "We can adjust it is position" wouldn't make sense; **its** indicates that **position** belongs to the **rug**.

15) The patient **lay** down for a nap half an hour ago. He was not feeling **well** after he received his shot. Notes: Use **lie** to mean "to rest" without an object; what may seem confusing is that **lay** is the simple past tense form of **lie**. Use **well** (not **good**) when it relates to health or wellness.

16) She **laid** her notebook on the table and opened the refrigerator. Unfortunately, **there** was nothing **good** to eat.

Notes: Use **lay** to mean "to place" with **notebook** as an object; **laid** is the simple past tense form of **lay**. "They are was nothing good" wouldn't make sense; "their was nothing" also wouldn't make sense because **their** indicates a sense of belonging. Here, **good** is a postpositive adjective (it comes after the noun **nothing**).

Made in United States
North Haven, CT
03 August 2022

22118899R00098